Dedication

To
Mark, Abby, and J. Mark
Ann and Al
Al III
Kes and Sam
Gloria and Jim
and
Jill
. . . my family.

SMALL STEPS TO BIG CHANGES

THE
7
MINUTE
DIFFERENCE

Allyson Lewis

PUBLISHING

New York

© 2008 Allyson Lewis

Published by Kaplan Publishing, a division of Kaplan, Inc.
1 Liberty Plaza, 24th Floor
New York, NY 10006

Printed in the United States of America

2009
10 9 8 7 6 5 4 3 2

ISBN-13: 978-1-4277-9794-0

Kaplan Publishing books are available at special quantity discounts to use for sales promotions, employee premiums, or educational purposes. Please email our Special Sales Department to order or for more information at kaplanpublishing@kaplan.com, or write to Kaplan Publishing, 1 Liberty Plaza, 24th Floor, New York, NY 10006.

Contents

. . . .

Acknowledgments

Books are not really written with pen and ink, nor are they simply typed on a keyboard. The words read here grew in my heart and came to life with the help of many friends and supporters. I'd like to thank all of them here.

First, I want to acknowledge my God for all the blessings he has given to all of us. There is no greater gift than His son, Jesus Christ.

Next, I thank my husband, Mark Lewis, and my children, Abby and J. Mark, for the joy they bring me. Love from your family gives you the freedom to dream, to grow, and to believe that you can be different tomorrow than who you are today. They are my inspiration and from them I learn what true love really is. I also thank my parents, Ann and Al White. Their love and support stands tall in my soul.

Susan Naylor has been my friend and co-worker for the past 12 years. She was a major contributor to this project. While I write about 7 Minute Ideas and micro-actions, Susan has taught me many of these concepts through the way she lives and works. I want to express my gratitude to her for all of her encouragement and inspiration.

Other friends who helped with this book include: Laura Allen, Lauren Appleby, Karen and Michael Berry, Cindy and Bill Brown, Tenny and Eric Brown, Jennifer and Max Dacus, Donna Evans, Jama and Wallace Fowler, Jeanne and Dave Grossman, Grant Hinkson, David Herdlinger, Sharon and Glenn Jones, Nellen and Steve Jones, Laura and Keith Kessinger, Dr. Florence Krause, Corley Madden, Vicki Massengill, Richard McKeown, Sharon and Harris Milligan, Barbara Reinhart, Bob Riley, Amy Tyler, Jeanne and Les Wyatt.

Additional friends and business associates who have had a profound impact on my life include: Jeff Adams, Greg Allen, Mike Arundel, Olin Atkins, Emily Bach, Paul Baranivsky, Ray Basile, Bob Bass, David Bettis, Mag Black, Mimi Bock, Doug Brown, Michael Burke, Connie Chartrand, Kathy Comerford, David Darst, Christi Edwards, Robert Fort, Christin Galloway, Paul Green, Raj Gupta, Ray Harris, Peggy James, Henry Kaplan, Larry Karban, Jack Kemp, Nancy Kennedy, Laura Ladrigan, Lynn Lindsay, Todd Locicero, Joe McAlinden, George McLeod, Scott McLeod, Mitch Merin, Wendy Moy, Greg Powell, Normajean Practico, Al Ragsdale, Rick Sanchez, Bert Simon, Ray Smesko, Colin Stewart, Rebecca Stilwell, Ben Tarantino, Rondi Thornton, Kathy Tully, Laura Van Orden, Dan Vacca, and Jeff Welday.

One of the best parts of writing this book was having the opportunity to work with Lorna Gentry. Lorna has been a writer for as long as I have been a financial advisor. I want to thank her for her advice, suggestions, friendship, encouragement, and expertise.

Many wonderful people at Kaplan Publishing have worked closely with me to make this book a reality. For their wise counsel and guidance throughout the project, I thank Cindy Zigmund, Leslie Banks, Courtney Goethals, Eileen Johnson, April Timm, Agnes Banks, Julie Marshall, Leah Strauss, Caitlin Ostrow, Daniel Frey, Maureen McMahon, Roy Lipner, and especially my editor, Michael Cunningham.

Finally, I want to thank those of you who are brave enough to believe that change really does happen in an instant. You are the real reason I have written this book. Keep "GROWING" and may God bless you.

Allyson Lewis
Jonesboro, Arkansas
2006

Introduction

A few years ago, during an annual team-building meeting at the brokerage firm where I work as a financial advisor, my team participated in an exercise in which we took a blank sheet of paper from a yellow legal pad and wrote five words at the top of the page. Those five words were, "My purpose in life is . . ."; with a 15-minute time limit, we were to write down the description to complete that thought.

As the clock began ticking, my mind drifted lazily through a variety of dreams and goals I'd aspired to over the years; then, my thoughts wandered back to the present, and the work I had waiting for me back in my office. By the time I snapped my attention back to the task, a glance at the timer told me that I had daydreamed through 8 of the 15 minutes. Then, as if out of nowhere, the words came to me. I wrote:

> "My purpose in life is GROWING. In life, I want to grow and change. I want to be different tomorrow than I am today. I want to grow as a wife—to be more in love with my husband, to hold hands more often, to enjoy

long talks late into the night, and to share our hopes and dreams. I want to grow as a mother—to watch my children mature into their own destinies. I want to grow as a spiritual person—to become kinder, wiser, more hopeful, and more understanding. I want to grow my skills as a financial advisor and help my clients grow their assets. I want to work at my job with joy and honesty and integrity. I want each day to be filled with fun and excitement and challenge. And, I want to help others bring about meaningful changes in their own lives, by sharing my discoveries and ideas. My purpose in life is fulfilled by growing and through helping others grow."

The timer went off and I looked up at my team members feeling slightly stunned. The preceding seven minutes had encapsulated a defining moment of my life. *The 7 Minute Difference—Small Steps to Big Changes* is a product of that defining moment.

Understanding the 7 Minute Difference and Micro-Actions

At the time I just described, I had spent 21 years of my life working in my vocation; I came to work every day and did a good job. But something was missing. I wanted more—more hope, more joy, more fun, and more fulfillment. I wanted to *be* more. I wanted to help others find hope, joy, laughter, purpose, and passion in their own lives. In just seven minutes, a simple exercise had helped me reach a whole new understanding of who I was and what I wanted to be. Working with just a kitchen timer, a legal pad, and an ink pen, I had given shape to an idea of my *purpose,* and that idea would help determine and guide the actions that have defined my life from that day on. Over the next several days I kept thinking about the power of those seven minutes. I realized that there were hundreds of things I could accomplish in seven minutes—tiny little opportunities to make my life and the lives of those around me better. I began to look at life through the lens of the 7 Minute Difference. The ripples of that idea are still widening, as I continue to grow in my purpose and passion for life through an ongoing series of small changes.

The subtitle to this book is *Small Steps to Big Changes.* I believe that small steps truly can bring about the biggest changes in our lives. The best part of all is that change happens in an instant—the moment you decide that, you truly *want* to be different. That is at the heart of my message. Change, in fact, is the essence of all life—without change, we die. Of course, most of us would like to make positive changes that represent growth and development, rather than decay. The problem is that we are uncertain of what the nature of those changes should be and what concrete steps we can take to achieve them. Too often, we think of change as being complex, unmanageable, and beyond our grasp. When we think that way, we ignore the fact that the biggest, most meaningful, and dramatic differences in our lives—and in our world—are really just the result of a series of small, seemingly insignificant changes. When changes are guided by our idea of purpose, they can build, over time, toward meaningful growth and development.

That understanding formed the basis of the first 7 Minute Idea I'd like to share with you:

· · · · ·

I believe that making even small changes in your actions and behavior can result in monumental differences in your life.

· · · · ·

In this book, I call the activities that result in these small changes *micro-actions.* Micro-actions are so simple they are often overlooked and underutilized. They are the tiny choices corporate executives and salespeople use every moment of every day to make the difference between mediocrity and excellence. In my experience, the micro-action of writing down a short description of purpose resulted in a major change in my personal and professional life, but micro-actions can take any number of forms, including:

- Outlining a daily plan of action

- Taking time to thank a co-worker for a job well done

- Building time into the day to catch up between meetings

- Being on time or early for every meeting

- Handwriting thank-you notes to two customers a day

- Reading ten pages of a book

- Getting up 15 minutes earlier

- Eating more fruit and drinking more water

When incorporated into a daily routine, these micro-actions take on even greater potential for bringing about immense new levels of productivity and growth in our work and home life. Although individual micro-actions might take 5 minutes, 7 minutes, 10 minutes, 15 minutes, or more, all of them are inspired by what I call 7 Minute Ideas—ideas founded in our purpose and passion that help us plan and carry out concrete steps toward the goal of making an important difference in our lives.

Why "seven minutes"? Studies have shown that the average corporate executive has an attention span of seven minutes. Further, according to Harvard psychologist George Miller, the brain is limited to remembering only seven pieces of information at a time. I know that my own attention can wander easily, so I wanted to create processes and systems for working through the day that were short and easy to implement. 7 Minute Ideas and the micro-actions that support them are my tools for maximizing my ability to succeed.

7 Minute Ideas are not just limited to identifying micro-actions that contribute to professional growth. I use these tools to grow personally, as well. For example, in around seven minutes I can

- outline and prioritize my top personal goals;

- write a description of where I want my life to be in five years;

- write a love letter to my spouse;

- call my parents;

- talk to my children about their day; or

- take a moment to relax and breathe.

Just seven minutes. What could you accomplish in seven minutes? I encourage you to begin to look at life through the possibilities of the 7 Minute Difference, and realize that in a very short period of time, you can use micro-actions to bring about monumental growth in your personal and professional life.

Why I Wrote The 7 Minute Difference

As a financial advisor, I work with a major New York brokerage firm. I have been in the same career since 1982, and with the same company since 1984. I loved my job since the first day.

Yet, as you can imagine, the past five years have been a challenge for all of us in the financial services industry. After almost two decades of spectacular growth in the stock market, between 2000 and 2002 we faced unprecedented events: the bursting of the technology bubble that resulted in a NASDAQ drop of 78 percent; the September 11 terrorist attacks; and the corporate scandals surrounding Enron, WorldCom, and Adelphia, which accompanied a 48 percent decline in the S&P 500 Index. As 2002 came to a close and 2003 dawned, I knew it was time for a change. A wise man once told me, *"Allyson, you can't choose to remain the same and expect your life to change. If you want your life to be different, you must be different."* Although that seems like common sense, far too many of us wake up every morning, repeat the very same motions we made the day before, and wonder why our lives remain the same.

In 2003, after realizing my first monumental 7 Minute Idea, I decided it was time to be different. With the realization that my purpose in life was all about *growing and helping others to grow,* I began to map out a business plan that aligned with my personal goals and values. But, I could not complete this process alone. I work as part of a three-person team at my firm, and together the three of us created team goals. In addition, we began to focus on strategic clarification. We designed systems. We increased our core competencies. It took almost all of 2003 to create the written strategies and processes we were going to implement in our daily business models.

As my team took the road map we had created and began to live it, 2004 became a magical year for us. Not only did our team's business grow by 67 percent in one year, but the level of satisfaction among our team members and clients began to rise geometrically. As our successes grew, I realized that the processes we were using—processes based upon my own ideas for making a difference in my personal life—had the potential to help others realize the same kind of positive change and growth in their own businesses, homes, and family lives. This book, *The 7 Minute Difference—Small Steps to Big Changes,* offers a blueprint for the processes of assessment, growth, and development we created.

Who This Book Is For

This book is written for businesspeople who want to believe that change really can happen in an instant. It is written for corporate executives, team leaders, insurance executives, financial advisors, salespeople, customer service associates, and human resource executives. It is written for accountants, attorneys, doctors, nurses, and teachers. This book is for all people who truly want to make meaningful changes in their professional and/or personal life, and who are willing to undertake the self-examination and small actions necessary to bring about that change.

The framework for this book contains several underlying truths:

1. Change begins to happen the moment you decide to change.

2. You must want change.

3. You must expect change.

4. You should enjoy the process of change.

You can be different tomorrow than you are today. Are you living from your heart? Can you feel that same level of passion and desire that first drew you to your current vocation? If you find yourself wanting to take a fresh look at discovering your hopes and dreams, then *The 7 Minute Difference* is the book for you.

What The 7 Minute Difference *Can Do for You*

Many of you have known for a long time that you need to make some significant changes in your life. Perhaps you've wanted to be more productive at work, receive a promotion, or even move into a new career. You might want to organize your home life or use better judgment in managing your time. You want to find time to do the things you believe to be most important in your life—to regain control over your health, finances, and other aspects of your life that feed your body, mind, and spirit.

The 7 Minute Difference offers a series of proven ideas that you can use to bring about those important changes. In this book, I'll share with you some of my favorite 7 Minute Ideas and the micro-actions that can bring those ideas to life. I will also outline projects that, with some thought and deliberation, you can leverage to effect meaningful change in your routine habits and actions. This book is filled with hundreds of specific, concrete, actionable ideas that you can begin to implement immediately in your daily life. You will learn specific techniques for

- discovering your purpose;

- changing your life through 7 Minute Ideas and micro-actions;

- choosing success;

- exceeding your customers' expectations;

- building momentum into your business;

- breaking through to your destiny; and

- translating life-changing decisions into life-changing actions.

This is a book about fulfillment of purpose. It doesn't just tell you about other people's successes; instead, it guides you in a step-by-step journey toward your own personal and professional destiny. I will show you simple, proven techniques for increasing your personal knowledge and raising your core competencies. I will guide you in establishing written goals that can outline a road map to your success. You will also learn powerful techniques for mastering core business practices, such as improving customer service, creating a strategy for growing your business, leveraging your key strengths, and overcoming critical weaknesses. Finally, this book encourages you to look for the best in life—both at the office and at home. My goal in writing this book was to help you rediscover the sheer passion and joy of doing what you do best. Above all, this is a book of hope.

Some Words of Encouragement from The 7 Minute Coach™

In addition to serving as a financial advisor, I am also a professional speaker and business coach to thousands of people. Many of the ideas presented in this book have grown out of the workshops and training classes I have taught across the country. Having taught the ideas you're about to discover in this book, I am now called The 7 Minute Coach™. In that role, my personal mission is to educate, motivate, and encourage others. That is what a coach does. Like a personal trainer who works right beside you, a good coach is always on your side, cheering you on and pushing you to succeed. A coach cherishes your victories and shares your pain in defeat. Many people have been my coaches and my teachers over the years, and I am trying now to pass along the great wisdom and support I gained from those kind and loyal mentors. Through them, I have understood that growing is a process, learning is a gift, and each day is a blessing filled with opportunities beyond our wildest imaginations. As you read this book, I hope you hear me whispering to you my friend and advisor's words of wisdom: "If you want your life to be different, *you* must be different."

What holds you back from becoming the person you want to become? What if that obstacle could begin to crumble in only seven minutes? Today is the day to stand on the edge of life with a new sense of determination and hope. As you read, I know you will come to understand that the first step toward monumental change truly can happen in an instant—and, it can happen to *you.*

1

. . . .

Discovering Your Purpose— and Passion

In the introduction to this book, I told you about a life-changing experience I had in 2003. It was then, during a simple team-building exercise, that I actually discovered and defined my purpose in life. Since that day, I have accomplished more personally and professionally than I ever dreamed possible. When we acknowledge and pursue our passion, when we pull our purpose into razor-sharp focus, we do more than just leverage bits and pieces of our past. We begin to plan our daily actions with the pursuit of passion and the achievement of purpose in mind. A simple seven minute exercise made my life different; that experience proved to me that, in an instant, change could happen.

This chapter helps you gain a clearer picture of your life's purpose, so that you can take the first steps toward monumental change. A clear statement and understanding of your purpose will form. You also will understand how the goals, dreams, choices, priorities, beliefs, and strengths you hold within you can help—or hinder—your pursuit of that purpose. Once you truly discover your purpose, life will never be the same for you; it will only grow better with each passing day.

The Power of Purpose

Sir Ernest Shackleton, one of history's most daring navigators, was a man whose purpose was to lead explorations of the earth's unknown areas. In pursuit of that purpose, Shackleton determined that he would lead an expedition to explore the Antarctic. He knew that the area held a wealth of important scientific information, and that such an expedition would be both historically and scientifically significant. He had a vision, he had a purpose, and he had a burning desire to accomplish things that no man had ever accomplished.

Shackleton and a crew of 26 men (and one stowaway) set sail from Plymouth, England, on August 1, 1914, aboard the *Endurance,* a ship named for the Shackleton family motto "By Endurance We Conquer." After sailing around the tip of South America, the ship slowly made its way through the thickening ice of the Atlantic Ocean until the crew could see the Antarctic continent before them. Then, on January 19, 1915, the ship stopped completely as the huge ice floes that clogged the sea trapped it.

With no other perceived options, Shackleton decided to wait until the spring thaw. Throughout the long, dark Antarctic winter the ship was locked in place, the men stranded. As a leader, Shackleton knew that he must keep the crew's spirits high or they would never be able to endure the horrible cold and loneliness of this desolate situation. He led the men in games of football and hockey on the ice. They celebrated holidays, sang patriotic songs, and raced their dog sleds in what they called the Antarctic Derby.

After ten long months, the ice floes began to shift; but instead of freeing the *Endurance,* they slowly crushed the ship and dragged her to the bottom of the ocean. The crew unloaded as many supplies as they could, salvaging food, lifeboats, sled dogs, and supplies, then made camp on the ice floe that had crushed their ship. If you have ever felt trapped by circumstances beyond your control, adrift, or crushed by the shifting changes of the world around you, you might have some concept of the challenges facing Shackleton and his crew during these agonizing months.

Again, Shackleton stepped forward as a leader. He gave his men his word that he would return every one of them safely to England. He did not allow them to consider the possibility that they would fail. Shackleton assigned daily rotating duties to the men, to keep them all engaged and actively at work on achieving their purpose. He reminded the men frequently of their return voyage, and he kept their dreams of home always vivid in their minds. He asked the men to describe their homes; the counties where they lived; their wives, children, parents, and friends. He treated the idea of a successful voyage home as a foregone conclusion, and made the goal of achieving that dream the driving force behind every crew member's work and purpose.

On April 12, 4 months after the breakup of the *Endurance,* the ice floe on which the men were camped broke free and drifted within 30 miles of tiny Elephant Island. In a courageous dash, Shackleton and his crew boarded their three tiny lifeboats and sailed for the relative safety of the island. Amazingly, all three boats landed safely. Although they were able to shelter in the inhospitable place, the only source of food on the island was its flocks of penguins. Shackleton knew that without vegetables, he and his men would contract scurvy and die, and he was determined to avoid such a horrible conclusion to their venture.

So, in a 22½ foot lifeboat named *The James Caird,* Shackleton and five of his men set out to make the whaling station on South Georgia Island, a 25-mile-long strip of land 800 miles away, across the open and stormy sea. With nothing more than a compass to guide them, Shackleton and 5 other crew members accomplished one of the greatest navigational feats in history and landed on the southern coast of the Georgia Island on May 10, just 17 days after launching.

Leading his tiny crew over uncharted mountains, through an icy rushing stream, and down the 30-foot drop of a waterfall, Shackleton successfully reached the whaling station within 36 hours after landing on the small island. Then, after 4 months of repeated efforts to return, Shackleton successfully sailed back to Elephant Island and rescued his remaining 22 crew members. When he landed back on the island, 105 days after leaving, he was amazed to find that all of his men remained alive. As Shackleton had promised, he and his men realized their dream; all of them returned to their homes in England. These were ordinary men with the same dreams and fears we have, but, by sharing the deep and passionate purpose of their leader, they persevered in the pursuit of an incredible achievement. Shackleton and his crew formulated common goals, and made sure that every choice they made and every action they undertook specifically moved them closer to those goals. They drew upon their strengths to survive throughout enormous hardship. Shackleton's core belief in a single, powerful dream guided them.

This story of courage and survival teaches so many lessons. What circumstances are crushing you? Are you making concrete plans to overcome them? Are you reaching out to your "crew" for encouragement? Are you willing to do whatever it takes to make it back alive? One of the most telling parts of Shackleton's story is his family motto, "By Endurance We Conquer." Too many people simply give up. Take courage, persevere, and never be afraid to follow your dream.

Acknowledging Your Goals

Your purpose tells you what you want to do with your life and how you want to serve others. As you learned in the story of Ernest Shackleton, your goals closely link to your purpose in life because they describe what you want to accomplish in the pursuit of that purpose. When you have a clear vision of your goals in life, you are one step closer to fully understanding and fulfilling your purpose.

Goals can be personal or professional, tiny or grand; achieved tomorrow or aimed at achievements extending past your span on earth. Consider, for example, the variety of my own goals:

- Personal goals—I want grow in my faith. I want to spend more time with my children, my husband, and my parents. I want to take more pictures of my family.

- Financial goals—I want to be debt free, contribute a set amount to savings each month, and increase my income significantly, all within the next year.

- Small goals—I want to clean my kitchen drawers and clear my closets of clutter, donating clothes we no longer wear to charity.

- Far-reaching goals, as well—I want to spread the message of hope and growth to millions of people. I want my workshops and books to touch so many lives that Oprah Winfrey invites me on her show.

- Vocational goals—When I'm at work, I want to work. I want to attract a very specific type of client, and I want to build a stronger reputation in the community and industry. I want to help people become better stewards of their financial resources, so they can enjoy life more and worry less about their money.

- Health goals—These are straightforward: I lost 11 pounds after my 44th birthday and I want to maintain my weight.

- Goals for leaving a legacy—I want to fund an endowment through contributions to a local university, to help reduce the tuition costs and other expenses of students with limited financial resources.

Micro-Action: Writing a Daily Goals List

Acknowledging your goals is essential to understanding your purpose, but it's only the first step toward achieving them. In his book, *Goals—How to Get Everything You Want*

Faster Than You Ever Thought Possible, Brian Tracy encourages readers to do three things:

1. *Write down your goals.* It's not enough just to have a vague idea of what you want to achieve; you need to develop specific goals and write them down.

2. *Make plans to achieve your goals.* For every written goal, you need to determine three or four specific actions that will help you reach that goal.

3. *Work on those plans every day.* Most goals cannot be achieved by sporadic and occasional effort, but require daily attention and action.

Tracy's book lays the groundwork for one of the specific 7 Minute Ideas I want you take away from this chapter:

· · · · ·

Your goals in life reflect and help fulfill your purpose.

· · · · ·

To support that idea, I encourage you to adopt this micro-action:

Micro-Action
· ·
Spend 15 minutes every day writing down your list of goals and two or three specific actions for achieving them.

FIGURE 1.1

Example of Allyson's daily goals

Personal Goals

1. I spend quality time with my husband & my children.
2. I plan ahead to make memories.
3. My children want me to "Be" with them, not just "doing" things. I enjoy just spending time "Being" together.
4. My house is clean & free of clutter.
5. I take more pictures of my family.

Health Goals

1. I weigh 117 pounds.
2. I enjoy eating healthy & nutritious foods.
3. I exercise 30 minutes 3 times a week, & I enjoy the time.

Financial Goals

1. I carefully review my income & expenses on a regular basis & make sure I am living within my means.
2. I reduce all debt outside of my mortgage.
3. I enjoy giving a percentage of my income to my church & other charities.

(Cont.)

FIGURE 1.1 (continued)

Vocational Goals

1. Our business increases by 30% this year.
2. We work from a process & system that help us understand our client's needs & is built on trust.
3. New clients call us regularly because we provide quality service to their friends.
4. We continue to attract large clients & we build friendships with them.
5. We focus on our strengths.

Legacy Goals

Family:

At the age of 85 I will have fulfilled my purpose when my husband still holds my hand in public, when my children know I love them & when my grandchildren think life is better for having me as a part of their lives.

Education:

I would like to leave a legacy for scholarships for student athletes at the collegiate level.

Faith:

I want to always be remembered as a person of faith, hope, encouragement & joy.

That's 15 minutes of work on your written goals, every day. If you could adopt this one micro-action, and take time daily to articulate plans for working toward your goals, what kind of changes might you make in your life? How might this single micro-action serve to differentiate you from your competitors? Statistics say that only 3 percent of Americans have any kind of written goals at all. Most of us talk a good talk. We *say* we want to be more knowledgeable, lose weight, clean up our house, or bolster our financial condition, but we *do* nothing to accomplish these goals. Just by the single daily act of acknowledging and affirming your goals, you vastly improve the likelihood that you will actually accomplish the goals you have set. Of course, you might find that your goals change over time, but that's okay; you can gauge your growth and progress by the changes in the goals you set for yourself.

Buy a notebook to record your top 10 or 15 goals. List the goals that will help propel you forward toward your purpose. Then use the list as a starting point for the daily micro-action of rewriting your listed goals, along with two or three specific steps for accomplishing them. Who do you want to help? Who do you want to serve? What do you want your legacy to be? Be specific in describing your goals and try to complete this list within 15 minutes.

FIGURE 1.2 My Daily Goals

1. _____

2. _____

3. _____

4. _____

5. _____

6. _____

7. _____

8. _____

9. _____

10. _____

11. _____

12. _____

13. _____

14. _____

15. _____

Aligning Your Choices, Priorities, and Dreams

In the process of pursuing my purpose in life, I've come to know that my success is decided by the choices I make, by the priorities I set, and by the dreams I cherish. The next 7 Minute Idea I want you to take with you is this:

· · · · ·

By aligning your choices, priorities, and dreams, you direct your actions toward achieving your goals and fulfilling your purpose.

· · · · ·

Feel the power in this idea. Every micro-action you take to support this idea will change you in meaningful ways and make you different tomorrow than you are today.

Micro-Action: Evaluate Your Choices

Right now is the time to consider—and even reconsider— the choices you have made and are making in your life. I know that our responsibilities dictate some of the choices that we make; we must earn a living and we must care for and nurture our families. Within those relatively broad boundaries, though, we make a wealth of other choices about how we live our lives. We choose what we eat, what time we go to bed and get up, who we hang out with, how we spend the money we earn, and how we spend our days. We choose how much and what kinds of television we watch, what we read, and where we get our information about current events. We even choose how we feel about ourselves.

Whether or not we acknowledge it, we also choose how successful we are in our jobs—how much we develop our skill sets, education, and training, and how far we grow as individuals. If you take time to learn how to use the latest technology that is available for your business, you have chosen to make yourself more valuable to your customers and in your workplace. If you leave work at 5:00 PM so you can catch your daughter's soccer game, rather than work late so you can have uninterrupted time at your desk, you've chosen to demonstrate your love and loyalty to your family. If you pass up the cookies and snack on raw vegetables instead, you've chosen to eat fewer calories and improve your nutrition.

Until you really acknowledge the choices you are making and the daily habits you choose to follow, you cannot fully appreciate the potential for change that your life possesses. You might feel that you are a prisoner of your responsibilities and that you have very little free time or freedom to choose. Yet if you consider the power of micro-actions and understand that even small changes can make a monumental difference in your life, you begin to realize just how much power your daily choices incorporate.

Use this micro-action to help become more aware of your choices and how these choices reflect your life's purpose and goals:

Micro-Action

· ·

Take seven minutes right now to review the goals you just listed and to record choices you will make, or have recently made, that reflect each of those goals.

Many of those choices will take the form of simple micro-actions. For example, when one of my goals was to lose weight, I chose to take the micro-action of joining Weight Watchers. If one of your goals is to save for your future, you might choose to take the micro-action of asking your benefits coordinator to increase your monthly 401(k) contribution by 1 percent. These tiny choices make a difference.

If you cannot remember a choice that supported an individual goal, can you remember a choice that actually worked against that goal? When you understand how often your choices support or undermine your goals and purpose, you become more aware of the power and possibilities of the small choices you make every day.

Micro-Action: Identify Your Priorities

Take a moment to consider your priorities, the things to which you are most willing to devote your time, energy, and attention. You can consciously choose your priorities and determine your actions based on them, or you can let unconscious actions and unexamined habits create priorities for you.

Some of those "accidental" priorities might be positive and worthwhile, many others will not be. By setting specific priorities, you take another important step toward aligning your actions with the goals you have set for fulfilling your life's purpose. As you work to bring about meaningful change in your life, remember this 7 Minute Idea:

· · · · ·

Your priorities reflect in the ways you spend the hours of your days.

· · · · ·

For example, if your health is one of your most important priorities, your choices and actions should contribute to good health. Are you going to bed and getting up at times that enable you to be well rested? Do you exercise and eat a healthy diet? If finding happiness in your professional life is an important priority, your actions should reflect that. Do you feel organized and capable of remaining on top of your work schedule? Do you manage your workday or is your life at the office in a constant state of chaos? Whether in your personal or professional life, your actions do determine your priorities.

Establishing priorities is a big step, but it actually involves a simple task. Try this micro-action, which can have big implications for your life:

Micro-Action

. . . .

Grab a blank sheet of paper and make a short, simple list of your life's priorities. Arrange them in order, beginning with the most important.

Ask yourself, "What things are most important in my life?" Here, for example, is the list I came up with:

1. Faith and spiritual growth

2. Family

3. Friends

4. Personal growth

5. Health

6. Vocation

7. Finances

8. Hobbies

As you can see, I did not take time to dig deeply into specific actions associated with these priorities. I simply took a few minutes to consider and list the things that I feel are the most important to me in my life. Now, complete the micro-action of listing your own priorities on the next page.

FIGURE 1.3 My Priority List

1. _____

2. _____

3. _____

4. _____

5. _____

6. _____

7. _____

8. _____

9. _____

10. _____

Now, hold the list in your hand, then look inside your heart, your calendar, and your checkbook and see if you are actually living a life that matches your priorities. Our priorities become the broad brushstrokes that form the outlines on the canvas of our lives. The choices that we make and the small micro-actions that follow those choices fill in those outlines with the color that paints the picture.

Acknowledging Your Dreams and Illusions

Dreams are amazing gifts. Our dreams can sweep us away to the farthest reaches of our imagination. Dreaming helps us to conceptualize our goals, so we can implement daily steps that draw us closer to realizing them. With the same power, however, our negative illusions can limit our lives and throw obstacles in our path toward growth and change. Consider this 7 Minute Idea:

· · · · ·

Our dreams influence our actions and therefore help form the blueprint of our lives.

· · · · ·

The brain is a mysterious force. The pictures we vividly place in front of our minds on a continuous basis often become self-fulfilling action plans. Our dreams are one of the strongest positive tools we have working in our favor—if we can dream it, we can become it. By taking just a short time to acknowledge the positive dreams we hold for our future, we strengthen our ability to achieve those dreams.

Micro-Action: Positive Dreaming

You can explore this idea by taking seven minutes (or five minutes, or a morning, or an entire weekend) just to dream about what your life could be like from this moment on.

Through dreaming, you form a clear mental image of your ideal life, and the things you do and experience within it. Take this simple micro-action:

Micro-Action

. . . .

Spend five minutes a day positive dreaming.

You will condition yourself to think and plan and act in ways that support the life you dream. Here is a simple exercise that can help you get started in this life-changing practice:

> Close your eyes for a moment and imagine a large, blank wall, eight feet tall and ten feet wide and completely white. The room is perfectly clean and in the back of the room is the most comfortable chair you have ever seen. See yourself sinking into its warmth and comfort as you pull a footstool under your feet. Take a few deep breaths, then begin to project a mental image on that clean, white wall of the life you want to be living in five years. What does the picture look like? Are you continuing to grow and learn more every day? Can you see yourself with new sets of skills and abilities? What is your family life like? Are you a homeroom mom or the coach of the soccer team? Those vacations you always talked about, do you plan and take them? What kind of relationships do you have with your friends?

Do they know you deeply and love you for the person you are? Take a moment to imagine your health. In your dream, do you maintain a healthy weight, exercise regularly, and eat the kinds of food that provide energy and strength? For a moment, dream about your job. Can you clearly see yourself in the promotion you always wanted? Can you envision how the dynamics of your leadership skills influence the future of your corporation? Consider your finances. Can you see yourself debt free and making more money than you are spending? Oh, it feels so good to have your finances back under control! Are you investing money for your future and giving to charity? It feels great to be helping other people and making a difference in their lives, doesn't it? Imagine all of these things as vividly as you can, and see yourself doing, being, and pursuing the life you want to have. When you have projected those pictures on the blank wall of your imagination, envision yourself standing up from your chair and walking toward them— becoming part of the life you have dreamed.

This blank wall is the canvas of your life and you are the painter. The brighter, the richer, and the more vividly you can paint this picture, the more likely it is to come true. If you practice this exercise regularly, your mind—both consciously and unconsciously—will guide you in making the decisions and taking the actions necessary to achieve your dreams.

Micro-Action: Breaking Free of Negative Illusions

Dreams represent our passions in life, and as such can propel us forward; negative illusions only serve to hold us back. I once read that the average person thinks over 400 negative thoughts about himself or herself every day. Our little brains go into motion and we think, "I am not smart enough. My hair looks funny. I cannot possibly do that. I am sure they will pick someone else for the promotion. I am too fat. I am too skinny. I don't make enough money. I can't. I shouldn't. I am scared." 400 times a day we beat ourselves up with these miserable thoughts. Subconsciously these fleeting ideas pop into our minds, destroy our self-confidence, and diminish our potential. These negative illusions might as well be called lies because they simply are not true. Other people do not share the negative illusions we have about ourselves, and those illusions do not come close to reflecting our gifts and talents. We just never give ourselves permission to explore how wonderful we really are. We need to look at ourselves from a different perspective and see ourselves in a different light.

Every day, I encourage you to explore this 7 Minute Idea:

· · · · ·

Your negative illusions do not define you.

· · · · ·

Try this micro-action to help take advantage of your uniqueness and reject those negative illusions you may have had all your life:

Micro-Action

. . . .

Set aside one specific time per day—for example while you are taking a shower or drying your hair—to concentrate on your dreams and the positive attributes you possess that will help you achieve them.

The negative illusions do not make you stronger and they will not help you grow, so they have no value to you as you work to make a difference in your life. Build instead on your dreams and strengths.

Differentiating Yourself through Your Core Convictions and Strengths

If I were teaching this chapter as a workshop on discovering your purpose, I would stop right here and ask the whole class what their core beliefs are about the work they do. Why? Because, your purpose in life ties to your core convictions about your life and work, and the strengths you draw from those beliefs.

Our core beliefs about our work must match our personal values. As a financial advisor, for example, I have these core beliefs:

- I can work with integrity.

- I can help people create comprehensive written financial strategies designed to achieve their financial dreams and goals.

- I can help people learn.

- I can do my work with honesty and joy and put my clients' interests first.

Core beliefs are important because we base them on our fundamental values, and those values form the foundation on which our future growth and success can thrive. In other words, we draw our personal and professional strength from our core convictions.

Micro-Action: List Your Core Beliefs and Strengths

Explore this 7 Minute Idea:

· · · · ·

In our private lives, our core beliefs are what make us individuals; professionally, our core beliefs differentiate us from our competitors.

· · · · ·

Now, take some time to consider and identify your core beliefs. You can break the process into simple micro-actions. Start by thinking about your strengths. Are you a good listener? Are you good in math? Are you a creative thinker? Are you caring? Are you a willing volunteer for school or charitable activities? In your professional life, are you the team leader, the delegator, or the visionary? Consider these questions.

Micro-Action

· ·

Now, take no more than seven minutes to list some of your most important strengths here.

Next, translate those strengths into statements of your core beliefs. For example, if one of your key strengths is your ability to build teamwork, you can state as a core belief, "I believe that I can build teamwork and help my team achieve more, as a result."

Micro-Action

. . . .

In the next seven minutes, list your core beliefs here.

_____

_____

_____

_____

_____

_____

_____

_____

_____

_____

_____

_____

Through two short micro-actions you have outlined your strengths and your core beliefs. You have described the qualities that make you unique—both as an individual and as a professional.

Micro-Action: Strengthen Your Competitive Advantage

Now, with that information in mind, how do you plan to *differentiate* yourself as an individual and your business within its marketplace? Please circle, underline, and highlight that question, because it leads to another incredibly important 7 Minute Idea:

· · · · ·

Differentiating yourself can propel you
to unimagined success.

· · · · ·

Everyone is gifted with unique talents, but only when we use those gifts to differentiate ourselves from our competitors can we truly succeed and move forward in our career. If you are a pharmacist reading this book, for example, how can your core strengths and beliefs make you different from every other pharmacist in your market area? All pharmacists can fill prescriptions, but great pharmacists differentiate themselves by the individual care and attention they give their customers. By caring about the sick people who come to you, listening to their needs, and by making sure that their prescriptions are filled correctly, you clearly differentiate yourself from your competitors who rush through business as usual.

What if you are a financial advisor reading this book? Your clients can buy stocks and bonds from almost anyone in the country. Many other advisors are well read, have a keen understanding of economic trends, and know how historical markets work. These are important strengths, but they might not be enough to convince clients to buy from you. Often, the strongest differentiators for a financial advisor are strategy and process. Great financial advisors are willing to take the time to use every resource at their disposal to research and discover products uniquely suited for their clients' interests, and they are confident that they will find those solutions. Beyond offering solutions to their clients, great financial advisors demonstrate confidence, and that confidence helps place the client at ease; every action of such an advisor helps increase his or her client's sense of financial security. Also, in any business, personal touches such as placing a follow-up call after a business transaction or providing regular progress updates regarding ongoing projects can make your service stand head and shoulders above that delivered by your competition. And some of the most meaningful and powerful differentiators for financial advisors have little to do with their business skills. These traits include trustworthiness, caring, compassion, and the ability to increase a client's confidence through education. Differences such as these may seem subtle to the individuals who offer them, but they shout loud and clear to the clients who benefit from them.

You can best differentiate yourself by expanding your strengths and improving your professional skill sets, whether they involve listening, researching, or learning new practices.

The first step toward this achievement can be completed in an instant.

Micro-Action

. . . .

Take a moment to list the areas you believe you can improve and strengthen your competitive advantage.

_____

_____

_____

_____

_____

_____

_____

_____

When you differentiate yourself through leveraging your important strengths and core beliefs, your clients sense those differences immediately. Understanding and using your core strengths and beliefs to set your services above others in the marketplace is another 7 Minute Idea that, through a series of micro-actions, moves you another step closer to being different tomorrow than you were this morning.

Unlocking Your Purpose through Action

If you needed proof that change can happen in an instant, I hope this chapter offered it. Consider for just a moment your latest accomplishments:

- You have acknowledged your passions.

- You have evaluated the important choices you make every day.

- You have set your priorities.

- You have examined your dreams and illusions, and learned an exercise for using your dreams to paint the canvas of your life.

- You have identified your important strengths and core beliefs.

- You have determined the unique skills through which you can differentiate yourself as a professional.

These actions can make fundamental differences in the way you see yourself, your life today, and the life you want to have tomorrow. Those differences now can serve as the springboard for even more growth, as you use the understandings gained to outline your purpose in life.

Micro-Action: Describe Your Purpose

For this chapter's final micro-action, I encourage you to run through your own version of the life-changing exercise I described for you earlier in this book:

Micro-Action

· ·

Take out a yellow legal pad, or use the space in Figure 1.4, and—giving yourself a set period of time—write down what you consider to be your purpose in life.

The ideas you have learned and the micro-actions you have accomplished in this chapter should make the process much easier for you than it was for me on that day back in 2003, but your result will be equally powerful. *Purpose is not about who we want to become, purpose is what we do for others.* Purpose is how you serve others with your gifts and talents. Keep this fundamental truth in mind as you write.

By outlining a clear and solid description of your purpose in life, you begin the process of fundamentally changing your attitude and approaches to your life—both at home and at work. Remember, "painting the canvas" is a process of discovering goals and determining what we want our lives to look like. What we do for others, however, defines our purpose in life. Deep within your soul drives your purpose, and

your purpose will likely revolve around your natural passions
and the things you love. I hope you will take the time to discover your purpose by completing this most important
micro-action.

FIGURE 1.4 My Purpose in Life Is . . .

_____

_____

_____

_____

_____

_____

_____

_____

_____

Embracing Change

We each have to take responsibility for our own destiny and do something different if we want to change it. You are not a prisoner of your past: Examine your choices, priorities, and dreams to help make decisions that can change your life forever. If your path is not working for you, change it. If you are in a job you hate, look for another job. If your marriage is faltering, do not just continue in misery; actively work together to understand and resolve the problems you face. If you are not the person you want to be, work to be different. As you strive to make meaningful changes in your life, be willing to step outside your comfort zone. If you want to make yourself more valuable within your profession, be willing to differentiate yourself by developing an area of expertise. Ask yourself what you need to do to develop expert skills in something that matters to you then make the decision to acquire those skills.

The surest way to achieve your dreams is to keep working toward fulfilling your purpose in life. Whether you realize it or not, your dreams are forever linked to your purpose. Now that you have a clear understanding of your purpose, you can begin to unlock that purpose through action. Though that task is monumentally important, it does not need to be overwhelming. In chapter 2, you will learn a number of 7 Minute Ideas and micro-actions that will help you fulfill your purpose by understanding your goals, increasing your activity levels, improving your organizational skills, and devising specific strategies for success. As you read the upcoming chapter, you will again learn that seven minutes can make a difference in your life, and that change truly does happen in an instant— when you make the decision to act.

2

. . . .

Expanding Your Possibilities for Growth—7 Minutes at a Time

In chapter 1, you learned firsthand the transformative power of small actions. Using only a few, simple 7 Minute Ideas and micro-actions, you built upon a series of changes in your understanding of your choices, dreams, strengths, core convictions, and unique contributions to arrive at a discovery of your purpose in life. That discovery supplies the foundation for everything you do from this moment on. Now, it's time to pick up your tools and begin constructing a future that fulfills that purpose and reflects your personal and professional dreams.

This chapter contains some of the tools—a builder's master set of concrete, actionable ideas that you can immediately use to improve your daily life. Here, I share with you 7 Minute Ideas and micro-actions that have propelled me along the path toward becoming more tomorrow than I am today. In the previous chapter, as you examined your unique strengths and contributions, you also highlighted some areas for personal and professional growth. The actions I describe for you in this chapter immediately trigger that growth, and many of them can be accomplished in a matter of minutes. Each of these tools help you build a strong and resilient framework of meaningful changes in your life—seven minutes at a time.

Breaking Boundaries—The Pumpkin and the Jar

Earl Nightingale tells a great story about a farmer who planted a field of pumpkins. He planted the seeds in hills, and over time they sprouted into vines and the vines burst into blossoms. He walked the field one day, admiring the many bright golden blossoms on his vines, and marveling at how

FIGURE 2.1

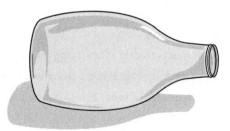

nature had transformed those tiny seeds he had planted into this glorious display in only a few short weeks. He never actually saw the plants grow, but they changed visibly every day. As he bent down to admire one particularly beautiful blossom, he happened to notice an old glass jar lying nearby, and he wondered what would happen if a pumpkin were allowed to grow only within the limited confines of that jar. He placed the glass jar over the blossom, walked away, and let nature take its course.

The months passed, and as harvest time drew near, the farmer again walked through his fields and took great satisfaction in all of the beautiful, ripe, round pumpkins growing there. Then, the farmer came across the jar, which he had forgotten about since he placed it over the pumpkin blossom so many weeks before. The pumpkin had totally filled the glass container, taking on the jar's shape and size—and then it had stopped growing. Although it was genetically capable of growing as large and as round as the other pumpkins in the field, the thin glass restraint had limited the pumpkin's growth and irretrievably altered its final shape.

The story of the pumpkin and the jar inspires me, because I know that all of us, at some point, have allowed artificial barriers to limit our hopes and dreams. I hope the story prompts you to consider what your possibilities for growth might be—how much potential for growth you have because of your natural intellect, curiosity, capabilities, and interests. Then, I hope you will think about what kind of artificial constraints you might have placed around your life—unnecessary barriers that are keeping you from achieving your full growth and, in the process, are altering the shape of your future.

Is negative self-esteem holding you back? Do you feel that the circumstances of your life make it impossible for you to grow into bigger dreams, ideas, and plans? Does this list contain barriers that you feel are holding you back in life?

- Lack of training, formal education, or certifications

- Lack of confidence

- Poor organizational skills

- Poor time-management skills

- Procrastination

I don't know what your personal barriers may be, but I can tell you that most of them—like every item in the preceding list—are no more substantial or necessary than the glass jar that confined the growth of the pumpkin. You can break free of your constraints to live a life with as much room for growth as your dreams can provide, and although breaking your barriers can open the path for life-altering growth, it doesn't have to be a painful or overwhelming task. The barriers only have as much power as you give them. I promise you that you can use the 7 Minute Ideas and micro-actions I offer here to break through those artificial limitations into a bigger life.

Using the Seven Minute Tools
for Fundamental Change

FIGURE 2.2

9.9.9.9.9

In an average workweek, we have, more or less, nine hours a day, five days a week, to do our job. That equals 45 hours. In that amount of time, we could get a lot done if we would put our heads down and work in a systematic fashion. However, few of us have the luxury of uninterrupted workflows and predictable, unchanging schedules. Meetings, telephone calls, e-mail, and a host of other daily interruptions are facts of office life for most of us. Not to mention, in view of the average businessperson's attention span, most of us lapse into mental vacations every seven minutes and then have to fight our way back to effective consciousness. So, to get the most from the hours of our days, we not only need to have a planned and systematic approach for tackling our daily jobs, we also need to be agile—ready to do whatever is necessary to deal effectively with life as it happens.

Developing a system, and dealing with shifting schedules and priorities, might require a fundamental change in the way you approach your daily life. Here are some 7 Minute Ideas that help change some of the fundamental processes of a daily routine to promote productivity and enable control over the hours of the day:

- Increase your activity levels

- Commit to daily contacts

- Develop a love of service

- Expand your knowledge

- Have fun

If you tried and failed at various methods for tackling the actions tied to these ideas in the past, you might feel that this kind of change is difficult to the point of being hopeless. Well, that's an illusion, and you may as well abandon it right now. The difficult challenges in life are those that help us grow; in that regard, these challenges are actually gifts. By the end of this chapter, you will have taken concrete steps toward accomplishing every one of the 7 Minute Ideas in the preceding list, and you will have done that by using a series of simple and effective micro-actions.

Micro-actions are one of your most useful and basic tools for growth. As you may recall from chapter 1, they are little acts that make you fundamentally different in 7, 10, or 15 minutes a day. 15 minutes of reading, 10 minutes of exercise, or 5 minutes spent jotting down a plan of action, I'm going to give you the information and skills you need to find out what will make the most difference for you.

One of my most important micro-actions limits the amount of time I spend watching the news each day. I want to remain updated on important events, without being overwhelmed with anxieties about the never-ending parade of negative news that fills the airwaves and printed page. My solution is to watch the top 15 minutes of headline news once every morning and again in the evening. That micro-action keeps me informed about the day's most important events, without sucking me into all of the gruesome and sensational details. With that limitation on news watching, I put my time to more positive use. If the news isn't an "addiction" for you, other equally draining television viewing habits might be stealing your day. Did you know the average American household watches five to eight hours of television per day? What a waste of time! If you do not have the time to finish all of your projects at the office, complete necessary chores around the house, or read a book that could change your life forever, could you make more time for those activities by spending less time in front of the television set? How much more could you accomplish in your life if you practiced the micro-action of limiting your television viewing to no more than one hour per day? That simple act could help you reclaim substantial amounts of lost time for use in activities that actually help you grow, both personally and professionally.

In the workplace, micro-actions are the small acts of attention to detail that transform your business performance from good to great. A five-minute follow-up call to check on a customer's satisfaction, seven minutes spent drawing up an action plan, three minutes to stop and thank a co-worker for her assistance on a project—these micro-actions might seem inconsequential, but they can fundamentally change your work performance, satisfaction, and success. When you learn to master the use of micro-actions in your daily business model, you become different in a number of subtle ways that result in taking *your* performance from "okay" to "excellent." How can micro-actions bring about change in your life? Compare the following two lives:

With Micro-Actions	Without Micro-Actions
1. Reads quality books on a regular schedule; studies to stay abreast of developments in his chosen industry	1. Chooses to be entertained by television rather than learn
2. Writes down personal and business goals every day	2. Writes down immediate "to do" lists only when forced, and bases all actions on immediate necessity rather than long-term goals
3. Lives with positive expectations	3. Complains that nothing ever "goes her way"
4. Has taken the time to discover his purpose in life and enjoys the passion that drives the fulfillment of that purpose	4. Has no clear understanding of purpose and no sense of how to serve others

5. Recognizes and works from personal strengths, all the while looking for ways to improve daily work habits

5. Looks for ways to make excuses for the poor outcome of projects, has sloppy work habits

6. Is a great team player, fun to work with, and a source of encouragement for co-workers

6. Has little or no motivation for going to work every day or doing a good job while there

7. Enjoys eating right, exercising, and is committed to following a healthy lifestyle

7. Lacks energy and spends "free" time watching television, shopping, and napping, rather than exercising

8. Constantly learns and explores new ideas and work methods; uses mentors, attends conferences and seminars to improve skills and knowledge

8. Has no desire to grow professionally

9. Prioritizes activities at work and makes choices accordingly

9. Deficient in organizational and time-management skills

10. Regularly remembers purpose and lets that purpose guide all activities—both short-term actions and the pursuit of long-term goals

10. Has no vision for the future of what she could become, not interested in developing a vision, no short-term work goals

Far too often people think they have to make some kind of sweeping about-face in their daily lives in order to accomplish real change. I disagree. I think people are reluctant to tackle change because at some time in the past they have attempted a major "leap" in their personal or professional behavior and fallen short. *Micro-actions are steps, rather than leaps—and steps are easy.* How hard is it to drink more water, eat some fruit every day, write down your top six or seven goals for the next day, or write a couple of handwritten thank-you notes to your employees or customers? The following sections describe a number of important micro-actions tied to accomplishing the 7 Minute Ideas listed above. If you decide to work on *just one micro-action a week for the next three months*, you will go through positive changes throughout that time. You can expect to experience positive changes in your energy level, in your attitudes, and even in your outcomes. At the end of three months, you will be a fundamentally different person than you were when you began. Growth fuels ongoing change and development that will continue throughout your lifetime.

Increasing Your Activity Level

Few people in this country today work on assembly lines, and most of us don't face a regimented daily workflow. After I complete a task, for example, I can wander down the hall to chat with co-workers or just sit at my desk and take a mental vacation before snapping back to action on another task. Answering phone calls, checking e-mail, attending meetings, conferring with co-workers on active projects—all of these activities are part of my job; but if I do not manage them carefully, they sometimes turn into time-wasting distractions.

Most of us are in control of how much—or how little—we accomplish in the course of our day with certain boundaries. Unfortunately, everything we *do not* accomplish in any given day adds to the backlog of work facing us the next morning. Unfinished business and unproductive work days leave us feeling stressed, frustrated, and inadequate, which is not a good recipe for professional growth. How often during your workday can you honestly tell yourself that the task you are doing at that moment is the most valuable way you could spend that minute, that hour, that afternoon? How many hours of your workday do you spend actually working?

If I said I would give you $86,400 every day for the rest of your life, but you had to spend it wisely or you would lose it, what would you do? Of course, you would do everything possible to spend the money wisely. Yet, each one of us is given 86,400 seconds every day and the same proposition challenges us; spend them wisely or lose them. You will never get back the hours you waste at work—that time is gone forever and leaves you with nothing to show for it. Time is the great equalizer; all beings on this planet have the same amount of time in their day. The way we *spend* that time, however, is often what separates the wildly successful people of this world from those who continue to struggle. Unproductive workdays are obstacles on your path toward professional growth.

This brings me to a 7 Minute Idea I'd like you to consider:

· · · · ·

To make a difference in your competitiveness, your performance, and your personal and professional success and happiness, you need to increase your activity levels, both at home and at work.

· · · · ·

If you increase your daily activity levels, you gain more benefit from every day of your life and move closer to achieving your goals and fulfilling your purpose.

This 7 Minute Idea became one of the simplest and most powerful forces for change in my life. To increase my activity level on the job, I came up with some specific micro-actions that helped me work with my head down and do my job with all the hope, energy, and encouragement I brought with me on my very first day of work. These micro-actions include:

- Making two additional calls per day

- Deciding to start and finish a project in the same day

- Working from repeatable processes and routines rather than reinventing the process every day

- Getting rid of the first of the day's distractions, such as a cluttered desk

- Determining never to leave the easy tasks unfinished

- Returning phone calls on the same day rather than letting them accumulate

- Working from a written plan of action

The sections that follow describe some of these micro-actions in more detail. These micro-actions will help you accomplish the same kind of fundamental change in your work-life that I experienced in mine; they will also serve as launching points for discovering your own seven minute tools for change.

Micro-Action: Create a Daily Written Action Plan

Here's a micro-action that just might become one of the best seven minute tools at your disposal:

Micro-Action

· ·

Every day, before you leave work, spend seven minutes writing down the top four to seven tasks you need to accomplish during the next work day.

Prioritize the items you list, so that you tackle them in their order of importance. As an example, on Tuesday afternoon at about 4:30 PM, I write down the seven things that I need to accomplish on Wednesday. Like this:

FIGURE 2.3

1. Send Excel spreadsheet to Susan for final review.
2. Talk to AW, TB, LT, CW, and LW about their portfolio holdings.
3. Call Steve Jones to initiate review process.
4. Write thank-you note to branch manager for his support of yesterday's client-appreciation event.
5. Discuss new client account-opening process at 9:00 AM team meeting.
6. Complete spring newsletter.
7. Send newsletter to compliance department for approval.

When I come in to work Wednesday morning, the list is there to guide me in tackling the most important tasks for that day. Writing a daily action plan is a simple, but powerful, tool for change; I *rarely* fail to accomplish everything on my list. If every day you have a written plan of action and start at the top and move right through each item in order, you will be *amazed* at how regularly you complete every task listed before the end of the workday.

Micro-Action: De-clutter One Area

Although you might not realize it, your organizational skills play a major role in your ability to increase your activity levels both at home and at work. Your organizational skills also affect the stress level or lack of stress you feel every day. The time you spend looking for lost items, sorting through clutter, trying to remember an important phone number, and following other habits of the chronically disorganized, is simply lost. I believe that it is important to have great organizational skills; not good ones, but *great* ones.

That said, I was not born with the "organization gene." The best investment I ever made was to spend an afternoon in my office with a personal organizational advisor. In four hours, we threw away mountains of paper, broken pencils, outdated files, dry pens, and assorted other useless clutter, then organized everything left into an efficient, pleasant working environment. In my organized office, I was more comfortable, confident, enthusiastic—and productive. Starting with that clean slate, I was able to use small amounts of time each day to maintain order in my work area. I improved my working environment and my productivity using one day's concentrated effort and a few minutes of daily maintenance activity.

Here is the important 7 Minute Idea that I want you to take away from this message:

· · · · ·

You can accomplish more, both at work and at home, if you can create and maintain an organized space.

· · · · ·

You do not need to hire a professional organizer (although I found that choice to be a good investment of both money and time). On your own you can take a day to label files, organize them, put everything where you can find it, and get rid of the things that you absolutely don't need. That stack of paper under your desk, throw it away. Even if you think you might need it later, throw it away, anyway. If it were important, it would not be in that stack under your desk. If you cannot take one full day to clear the clutter in your office, kitchen, or bedroom, start with a series of micro-actions.

Micro-Action

· ·

Spend 15 minutes each day clearing out one drawer, or devote 20 minutes of your weekend to sorting through two shelves in your storage closet. Schedule 10 minutes, three times a week, to work on your office files.

You will be amazed at how good it feels to work in an organized space, and how much more work you can accomplish.

Committing to Daily Contact

Another important 7 Minute Idea for growing professionally and personally:

· · · · ·

It is vitally important that you stay in touch with your clients or customers, patients, employees, and associates.

· · · · ·

No matter how you make contact—whether through a brief catch-up telephone call, a short e-mail, a handwritten thank-you note, or a periodic newsletter distribution—regular contact feeds and strengthens your business relationships, regardless of what business you're in.

Studies have shown, for example, that clients like to hear from their financial advisor between 12 and 20 times per year. Meeting this contact goal requires more than just a commitment to keep in touch with our clients. My team, therefore, adopted a systematic process for contact management. We use a database management system called ACT!, which records our contacts with our clients and alerts us when it is time to contact them again. We also contact our clients in a variety of ways; through our monthly newsletters and other electronic communications, through phone contacts, and through face-to-face appointments or teleconferences scheduled on a quarterly, semiannual, or annual basis. Finally, we host a few off-site events (picnics, educational presentations, and so on) to educate and thank our clients.

Your business and clients will have their own expectations for contact, but the key is for you to clearly understand and then meet those expectations. Ask your clients how often they would like to have contact with you and what kinds of contact they would prefer. Then, devise a plan for meeting those expectations. To support this idea, you can use this simple micro-action:

Micro-Action

. . . .

Set and keep a commitment to make a minimum number of customer and/or co-worker contacts each day.

Your daily commitment to contact will keep you actively engaged and in touch with the people who matter in your business. At the same time, an ongoing commitment to daily contacts makes you *different* than most of your competitors.

Developing a Love of Service

Committing to a practice of daily contacts is one of the fundamental habits that will help you develop a love of service.

The next 7 Minute Idea I want you to remember from this chapter is:

· · · · ·

You will be better in the work that you do if you develop a love of service.

· · · · ·

Serving others, whether through paid activities or simply through acts of cooperation, kindness, and support for mutual goals, is an act of joy and an essential ingredient for professional and personal growth.

Most of us begin working because we need to pay the bills, and that need is a strong enough motivation for a while. At some point, however, we realize our job means much more than a paycheck. Some of my happiest clients are school teachers, and I can say with great confidence that few school teachers in this country are "in it" for the money. The best teachers are those that have a strong love of service; as a result, the work they do extends beyond the classroom and lives on well beyond the last day of school. Do you remember your junior-high basketball coach? Who taught you to love reading? Good teachers stay in close contact with their students, checking on their progress, asking how things are at home, congratulating them on their big (and small) achievements. How much better will you be in your work if you engage actively with the people you serve?

Expanding Your Knowledge

The next 7 Minute Idea I want to discuss is this:

· · · · ·

To grow professionally you must increase your knowledge.

· · · · ·

Increasing my personal knowledge is now a lifelong quest.

Now is the time to do whatever it takes to become the absolute best in your field—the "go-to person" others turn to for expert advice and guidance. If the knowledge, skills, and information you offer your company are commonly available from many people, you do not add much value to the organization. If you are a middle-level manager, for example, what sets you apart from others in your job category? If you want to grow professionally, you need to grow your knowledge, skills, and information to take you beyond your current plateau. What skills would help you move from a $50,000 a year job to a $70,000 a year job, or from a $70,000 a year job to a $500,000 job? After all, there is no real physical difference between the $70,000 worker and the $500,000 worker. Like pumpkin seeds, they both share the same genetic makeup. The real differentiator between these individuals is the knowledge they hold and their ability to use it. Expanding your knowledge expands your potential for growth. I believe the choices here are simple: We grow or we die. We learn or we fall behind. I encourage you to choose to increase your personal knowledge.

Micro-Action: Reading Ten Pages a Day

What do you think of when you consider how you might increase your knowledge? Do you think of going back to school for an advanced degree or attending a two-week training course or a series of professional seminars and workshops? Those learning activities will help you expand your knowledge, and I strongly recommend that you take advantage of them whenever you can, but those activities are not micro-actions. They require significant investments of time, energy, and money. So if those investments are possible *occasionally* in our lives, we need to supplement them with learning opportunities we can make use of on a daily basis. The easiest, most flexible, and least expensive way to expand your knowledge is to become a reader.

If someone said they could give you a million dollars, would you take it? Yes, you would. Well, I'm telling you, I can give you a million ideas, and all you have to do is open a book. Let's say that you want to be wealthy beyond your wildest dreams. How do you do it? Why not read books on wealth or finance; read how other people achieved their wealth, and then use what you can of the lessons you have learned. Do you want to have a fabulously successful marriage? Do you want to be a leader in your business? Do you want to be someone who can change the world for the better? Each of these has thousands of books written about them and a multitude of other life-changing topics, and the knowledge these books hold draws from a wealth of experiences and perspectives. The information in books can nourish the seeds of change and growth that you hold within, and it is all just waiting for you in the local library or bookstore.

A love of reading runs like a common thread through the lives of the best, the most successful, and the most influential people our world has produced. Theodore Roosevelt is said to have read over 20,000 books in his lifetime. Abraham Lincoln would have had no opportunity to escape poverty had he not been a reader. (Did you know he primarily read while lying on the floor and he almost always read aloud?) As a young man, Benjamin Franklin was too poor to buy books, so he would borrow them from friends who were booksellers, then stay up until the wee hours of the night reading so he could return the books by morning. By the time he died, Franklin had accumulated over 4,000 books, building one of the largest private libraries in America.

The habit of reading is a powerful differentiator, too. Consider these startling statistics from the American Booksellers Association:

- 80 percent of Americans did not buy or read a book this year;

- 70 percent of American adults have not been in a bookstore in the past five years;

- 58 percent of American adults never read a book after high school; and

- 42 percent of university graduates never read another book after graduation.

Let that sink in . . . 58 percent of Americans will never read a book after high school! What a shame—and an opportunity for you to both make a difference in your life and differentiate yourself from your competitors.

I am not talking about carving out two or three hours every day for reading. I am telling you there is great power in the simple micro-action of reading ten pages of life-changing ideas and information every day. If you are truly ready to change your life forever, then you MUST become an avid reader. The idea of becoming smarter tomorrow than you are today should really make your heart pound. Do you read at least one nonfiction book a year? If you read ten pages a day, you could finish one 300-page nonfiction book *every month*. Are you willing to commit to reading ten pages of one nonfiction book each day? *What a simple concept: ten pages a day to change your life!* How different would you be next year if you read 12 phenomenal, life-altering books over the course of the next 12 months? How different would you be in 4 years if you had read 48 of those books in that time?

The Appendix of this book contains a reading list of some of my favorite titles, categorized by topic. Use this list as a starting place.

Micro-Action

· ·

Choose one book then commit to the micro-action of reading ten pages of it every day.

When you finish the book, you will have immediately differentiated yourself from *80 percent of all Americans.* You will have established the habit of reading—a habit that will change your life for the better in ways that you cannot even begin to imagine.

Micro-Action: Listen to Audio Books

My personal goal is to read one book a week. That's right, one nonfiction book a week. It is amazing to me how much I can learn by opening the pages of someone else's story and learning from their mistakes and successes. You are thinking, "Allyson, how in the world can you find time to read a book a week?" Well, I do read a lot. I try to read between 15 minutes and an hour before I go to bed. But I also have one other micro-action that helps me expand my knowledge:

Micro-Action

· ·

Listen to audio books on CD, tape, or an Apple iPod.

Yes, I use an Apple iPod, one of those technology gadgets you can master in a few short minutes. I also subscribe to a Web-based service called Audible.com that offers over 25,000 titles of major, mainstream books on audio. For a reasonable monthly charge, I can download two major titles per month onto my computer and then into my Apple iPod.

So all of those hours I spend in my car, going to and from the grocery store, going to and from work, I'm not listening to the news, which does me no good. I am not listening to the radio, which although entertaining does not challenge my mind. I am listening to books on tape about people whose lives have made a difference in this world. You do not need to buy an iPod or subscribe to a monthly audio book service. You can borrow books on tape or CD from your local library or buy them in the bookstore, and listen to them on a portable player while you are running errands, eating lunch at your desk, or doing chores around the house. This is another simple micro-action with powerful potential for growth and change.

Having Fun

My next 7 Minute Idea for taking a concrete step toward professional growth is this:

· · · · ·

You must have fun in your work if you want to grow within your profession.

· · · · ·

Your work occupies approximately one-third of your adult life. If you do not take pleasure, joy, and satisfaction from doing what you do for a living, you will not do it well nor will you find true success. The micro-action I recommend you use to support this idea is to find one way that you can improve your enjoyment at work every day. Make an extra effort to collaborate with the people at work with whom you enjoy working. Be the instigator of a monthly office potluck or find some way to turn a boring but essential task into something interesting and enjoyable.

That is what we did at my office during a day when our entire staff was having new computers installed. We knew without access to our computers it would be difficult to get much work done. Therefore, we handed out printed invitations to a "Back to the '70s office event." Each invitation came with a tie-dyed t-shirt, and we were all encouraged to wear the shirts with bell-bottom jeans instead of our usual business suits. The reason for this casual clothing was that we were going to devote the day to office de-cluttering and organization—a day to sit on the floor and deep clean our files and our desks. We may not have had computers, but we had a ton of fun and we all got a LOT of work done. Our branch manager even provided lunch from Sonic and we had cheeseburgers and chocolate malts delivered by roller-skating "car hops." With this simple idea, a day that could have been a complete loss transformed into a productive day laced with fun and memories that bonded us all together.

Another micro-action for increasing the amount of enjoyment you have at your office is to thank somebody for something every day at your office. That thank you can come in an e-mail, a short word in the hallway, or from a hand-written note. Thank a co-worker, thank your boss, or thank your direct reports; thank the person in the mailroom or the IT department representative who fixes your computer. However you do it and in whatever role, take just five or ten minutes every day to let the people you work with know that you appreciate their skills, efforts, and abilities, you will improve your relationship with each person that you thank, and by doing so improve your working environment. You will find that your work goes more smoothly, you get more cooperation and assistance from those around you, and that you have more opportunities to do more with the time you have at work. In short, you will have fewer frustrations, more fun at work, and be better able to grow and succeed during the time you spend there. Again, believe me that these small changes truly can make a big difference in your life.

Devising Your Own Strategies for Change

As we come to the close of this chapter, I would like to ask you to consider the ideas we've talked about and use them as inspiration for devising your own strategies for personal growth and professional success. Then, try this micro-action:

Micro-Action

· ·

Take the next seven minutes to write down ten strategies for action—five devoted to personal growth and five aimed at professional growth. List ten concrete actions you can take to grow or improve your current business model and to become different tomorrow than you are today.

Draw upon the 7 Minute Ideas you learned in this chapter, but do not limit yourself to them. The strategies you list in this micro-action can be as simple or as grand as you want them to be. Your strategies might include going to bed earlier, getting up earlier, eating two more servings of vegetables every day, reading 15 minutes a night, spending more time with your children, cleaning out one closet, clearing your desktop of clutter, or practicing one new work-simplifying technology for ten minutes every day for two weeks. Using the lines on the next page, take seven minutes to list these strategies right now:

Personal Action Strategies:

1. _____

2. _____

3. _____

4. _____

5. _____

Business Action Strategies:

1. _____

2. _____

3. _____

4. _____

5. _____

How will the above lists make you different? I would guess that less than 10 percent of the people reading this book would ever take the time to follow this micro-action of writing out these lists. However, 10 percent of my readers will have demonstrated that they are willing to do more than read about change, and they will have set in motion a whole process of ongoing change that will transform their lives. With these lists in hand, you now must make a commitment to *act on them every day* as the next step in your journey toward professional growth.

Such strategic activities are just part of the daily rituals of living that differentiate those who are successful from those who are not. Building upon this foundation, you have already begun the process of developing the larger attitudes and making the important choices that help you fulfill your purpose in life and reflect success in your very being. The next chapter will take you to the next level of change by offering you some 7 Minute Ideas for choosing success every day, in *everything* you do. You will create a vision that is exponentially larger than your current life, and you will be amazed at how quickly you grow to fill the possibilities of your expanded vision and dreams.

3

. . . .

Choosing Success—
Every Day

The preceding chapters helped you build a foundation and framework for a successful life. You learned that by working to expand your knowledge base, by setting and following specific strategies, and by committing to a daily action plan you set the stage for a successful business life. Upon that stage, the choices you make every day—the unscripted rituals and routines that make up much of everyone's life—also play an important role in your personal and professional successes.

Consider this: For the most part, life is a series of daily habits. That idea may sound simple, but it is also quite powerful. You often hear people talk about "the rhythm of life" when talking about nature—the changing seasons, migration, the cycle of birth and death. Well, the daily acts that make up your existence are part of the same rhythm. You wake up, get dressed and ready for work, and drive the familiar route to the office; you get your first cup of coffee, sit down at your desk, and begin the daily tasks that make up your workday. The ability to make the most of these daily rhythms—to use the ordinary habits of the day as a springboard for extraordinary achievements—strengthens humans, as it does every living thing. Even if we are recognized for our big achievements, we are defined by our daily routine.

You have probably heard people say that life's daily routines can be "crushing." I don't share that idea at all; I believe that daily routines can be empowering. Now, I do not think any of us should allow a rigid schedule or inescapable pattern to command our life. Instead, if you are in the habit of reflecting success in the small things you do every day, you are preparing yourself to be successful in the *unordinary* aspects of your day as well. By choosing the habits of success, we are much more able to deal with the unexpected challenges and opportunities we encounter as part of any active, growing, and changing life.

In this chapter, we focus on developing healthy routine skills, such as:

- Believing in your ability

- Communicating success through body language, clothing, and presence

- Networking to communicate a knowledge of your business *and* the customers you serve

Each of these skills contributes to the rhythm of a successful life. Think of them as the heartbeat of success, or as the background music that links and supports the action taking place on the stage of your daily existence. Once this heartbeat is strong within you, once you have learned the rhythm of success, you are primed for top performance. You can see opportunities that others overlook, and you can successfully deal with whatever life throws your way. This chapter offers concrete, specific 7 Minute Ideas and micro-actions that will help you build routines to make your life more workable—and more successful.

What I have learned as The 7 Minute Coach™, is that the simplest acts can make the biggest changes in your life. In fact, choosing to live a successful life is really a very simple choice to make, isn't it? Every small change that you incorporate into your daily life is a concrete step toward becoming different tomorrow than you are today; every monumental change is, in fact, the culmination of a series of small acts. The 7 Minute Ideas and micro-actions you read about in this chapter are, by design, simple; the effect of incorporating them into the daily rituals of your life is revolutionary. Let me give you some important advice right up front. As you read this chapter, whenever you see an idea that strikes you as being incredibly simple, stop right there, go back, and read the idea again—and again.

What is it that is holding you back? How are you painting the canvas of your life? Do you dress appropriately? Do you communicate your energy and abilities to your customers and co-workers? Do you make a habit of demonstrating how well you understand your business and the customers you serve? If not, now is the time to change your routines—and change your life.

Believing in Your Abilities

Here's the first 7 Minute Idea in this chapter:

. . . . .

Believing in your ability is the first step in moving to the rhythms of success.

. . . . .

Do you recall the discussion about the power of negative illusions? In chapter 1, we talked about the fact that, on average, we criticize ourselves *over 400 times* every day. The morning is prime time for us to start tearing ourselves down. We get out of bed and shuffle into the bathroom and—oh, my word, what is that looking out of the mirror? We get dressed and—wait a minute—does that waistband feel tighter than it used to? We're on our way to work, and—oh, no—the notes for this morning's meeting are still on the desk at home! Everything is wrong, and somehow it's all because we are overweight, not attractive enough, and too disorganized, and those are just the faults we notice in the first hour after we wake up.

If we were delivering those same unkind messages to anyone else that we know—our family, friends, or co-workers—what kind of an impact do you think our criticism would have? Would the people we insulted look fresher when they get out of bed tomorrow morning? Would they immediately start eating right and exercising more? Would they begin using a checklist every morning to make sure they did not forget a thing before they walked out that door? I think you know the answers to those questions. Harsh criticism does *not* consistently motivate or nurture most people. Change and growth occurs through encouragement and increased self-esteem. People tend to live up to (or down to) the expectations of others, and that truth is reflected in the power of the messages we give ourselves about ourselves. Negative illusions drag us down and put us out of step with the rhythm of success. We can achieve more when we have a fundamental belief in our abilities to do more.

In the late-1980s, I decided I needed a convertible, so I went out and bought a 1972 MGB convertible, bright red with a black convertible top. I thought that buying a flashy convertible would be a great way for a 29-year-old, single woman to meet a man. It turned out I was right. I did meet a man—my mechanic. This car needed a lot of attention, but it was a beautiful car, and I loved it. Driving home on those Arkansas spring afternoons with the car's convertible top down and the music blaring, I believed that life just could not get any better.

Now, I didn't feel that way on my very first day of driving the car; the car had a standard shift, and it had been years since I had driven one. I had faked my way through the test-drive, with some advice from the salesperson, and I knew the fundamental principles of driving a stick shift, but I had no recent practical experience doing it. I was completely unprepared, however, for managing a stick shift on the hilly streets of Little Rock, Arkansas.

I managed to make my way to the first stoplight without too many problems, but the stoplight was on an incline, and when I looked in the rearview mirror, I saw that another car had pulled up close behind me. I knew that if I did not want to roll backward into this person, when the light turned green, I would need to get my car into gear quickly. I started to sweat.

When the light changed, I did what any rookie stick-shifter would do; I let the clutch out all the way and gunned it. The car took one jerk forward, the engine went "vrmmff!" and died. I stalled cold at the intersection. At that moment, I had absolutely no belief in my ability to get that car moving again. I was so busy feeling embarrassed, inadequate, and panicky that I could not think of one useful thing to do. I wanted to get out of the car and run, but I was frozen in my seat, staring at the dashboard as if I had never seen one before.

Then, I looked in my rearview mirror and saw that the man behind me was laughing out loud, but at the same time, he was backing up to give me more room to get the car in gear and moving up the hill. That small act told me that he had no question I could drive that car through the intersection, and he was going to give me the room to do it. That was all it took to remind me that I *could* get the car in gear, I just needed to go about it differently. I started the engine then let the clutch out slowly while I gave it some gas. The transmission took hold, the engine went "ruhh, ruhh, ruhh, ruhh," and I lurched and sputtered through the intersection. It was hardly a pretty take-off, but I made it up the hill. All afternoon I practiced driving the car, and by the end of the day, shifting gears was a breeze; the less I doubted my ability to handle the shift, the fewer troubles I had with it. If I did stall, I did not panic; I just started the engine and tried again. I no longer thought about whether I was capable of shifting, I just knew that I was. I could drive my precious red convertible wherever I needed or wanted to go, and shifting those gears became part of the powerful experience of driving that beautiful car.

The great part about belief is that it creates reality; if you believe you can do something, you probably can. On the same note, if you tell yourself that some task is simply beyond your capabilities, then you fail before you even begin. Say that you are new in sales, and you are in front of a prospect for that very first time. Boy, you look good. Your hair is styled and your nails are trimmed. You have on your best suit, your tie is straight, and your shoes are shined. As soon as you open your mouth, though, out comes the equivalent of "Ruhh, ruhh, ruhh, ruhh." You are sputtering up the hill as I did in that shiny, red convertible. You stutter and stammer, your brow breaks out in a cold sweat, and you don't think you're going to make it. That is precisely the reason you are stalling; you did not go into the meeting armed with a fundamental belief in your abilities. Even worse, your prospect senses your confusion and lack of confidence, and walks away. Now, you do not just believe that you will fail; you *have* failed, and you have set the stage for a series of uncomfortable, unproductive client meetings down the road.

Remember, if you believe it, it can come true. Your customers can tell what you believe about yourself and your abilities almost immediately, and the customer is unlikely to second-guess your negative illusions. I assure you if I had a knee injury and I went to an orthopedic surgeon who was uncertain about what kind of care I needed, I would seek out another physician. If my accountant asked me, "I don't know, what do you think about claiming this deduction on your taxes?" that would not be a good sign either.

In business and in life, we must have total and complete faith in our ability to serve and help the people we are there to help. Learning any new skill is simply a matter of practice. I relearned to drive a standard shift in about half a day. Some of the skills you need for performing well in your job will be just as fast and simple to learn; others may take years of experience, but you *can* master any aspect of your work. Given three months, six months, or a year, just think how much better you can be at any of the crafts involved in your profession if you seek out opportunities to learn and practice them. Belief in your ability is the first step in moving to the rhythm of success in any aspect of your life.

Mastering Your Body Language

Body language is an area of study that many of us have heard of but have not really pursued. I am taking body language more seriously today than I ever have before, because I now know that it is the most direct way of communicating your abilities to others. Have you walked into a retail store only to find the sales clerk listlessly leaning against the wall with one leg bent and arms crossed over her chest? The message of that body language comes through loud and clear . . . "I am only being paid $6 an hour and now you've got the nerve to interrupt me by asking me to wait on you." On the other side, can you remember your body language when you were invited to attend a special event with someone you love? Throughout the evening you walked a little faster, you sat a little closer, and you made specific eye contact and held their gaze.

Controlling what your body language is saying to those around you and being able to read and interpret the body language of your clients is a skill you will want to master. Your understanding and use of body language affects your negotiating skills, your ability to sell, and your ability to win your clients' trust. Remember this 7 Minute Idea:

. . . . .

Improving your knowledge of how to read and understand body language can dramatically improve your ability to move beyond your current place in life.

. . . . .

There is an interesting study by Albert Mehrabian, Emeritus Professor of Psychology at University of California, Los Angeles. His research was based on interpersonal communication and, while the percentages wouldn't accurately apply to public speaking or group presentations, the implications are clear: non-verbal cues and tone affect how our words are heard and understood. The Mehrabian research shows that only 7 percent of the information people walk away with is the result of words that you have spoken. A full *55 percent* of their response to you forms from their perception of your body language and another 38 percent comes from your vocal quality.

Remember, people hear your words, but they mainly listen to you through a subconscious filter. They "hear" your eye contact, they "hear" your smile, and they "hear" your overall body language. Even if you whisper, your body language screams.

"Reading" Body Language

What is your body language saying to your employees, your co-workers, and your clients? What messages are your posture, your facial expressions, and your physical energy level communicating about what you are really thinking on the inside? Your body language speaks to a client, prospect, or patient ten times louder than any words you could ever say. So, when you greet your clients, make sure you are communicating your pleasure at meeting them with both your words *and* your body language. You want your body language to speak with excitement and your vocal quality to be upbeat and lively. If you are unprepared for the meeting or uncertain about your ability to successfully effectuate it, your clients will see and "read" the fear being communicated by your body language.

In his book, *How to Say It at Work: Putting Yourself Across with Power Words, Phrases, Body Language, and Communications Secrets* (Prentice Hall, 1998), Jack Griffin provides an intriguing "translation" of various body postures and their meanings. Based on his information and some of my own personal observations, here are some of the classic signals of fear that people communicate through body language:

- *Swinging legs, tapping feet, or otherwise being "fidgety."* Those types of movement spring from nervousness, and nervousness can be contagious. If the people we meet sense we are nervous about our performance, they, too, will grow nervous about it and suspect we are inadequate for the job.

- *Crossed arms.* Crossed arms express an unwillingness to move forward, we subconsciously use our crossed arms to protect our vital organs. Crossed arms also communicate insecurity. If we are presenting ideas to our prospects, and they cross their arms, their body language is telling us to back up, slow down, and take them through the information again.

- *Twirling the hair or making aimless hand gestures.* Playing with your hair (something women do more frequently than men) also sends a message of insecurity, as does waving the hands about in meaningless gestures. When speaking, we should use our hands to make strong gestures that accentuate important points within the information we are delivering.

- *Lack of eye contact.* Darting eyes can make others feel that you aren't focused on them or that what you're saying isn't believable. Remember the last time you were at a dinner party and the person you were speaking to kept looking all around you while you were attempting to hold a conversation with them. Their lack of eye contact, made you feel unimportant. Looking down at the floor while speaking to someone can communicate a lack of confidence in yourself and your thoughts.

- *Biting or repeatedly licking the lips.* When I get nervous I bite my lip, which just screams my nervousness to the people I am speaking with. Our face should always reflect the message we are delivering—animated, engaged, sincere, and confident.

- *Open palms/closed palms.* Palms tell a lot about a person. Open palm gestures reflect openness and a willingness to help, whereas a closed fist suggests a need for authority. When people hide their palms behind their back, they may be hiding the truth. When shaking hands with someone, a palm up handshake implies a welcoming spirit and submissiveness, while a palm down handshake may indicate a need for dominance.

- *Touching the mouth, nose, or chin.* When clients touch their mouth or chin and say, "Yes, I'll get right back to you on Tuesday," they might not actually be planning to get back in touch with you on Tuesday, or at all. When people cover up their mouth, their body language says they are covering up the truth. If a speaker touches or begins to scratch their nose, they may also be signaling that they are not telling the truth. You can see this phenomenon at work in your own communications; if you catch yourself telling something you are not completely sure about, notice that your face begins to itch somewhere. I cannot explain this phenomenon, but I am glad to know about it. To make sure your body language conveys the honesty of your words, keep your hands away from your face.

Your body language conveys your energy to those around you. Energy and excitement is what fills leaders. Without saying a word, they can inspire those around them with potency, life, and hope. Body language affects how everyone you meet and speak with during the day responds to you. By becoming aware of your own body language, and using it to communicate the message you *want* to deliver, you become a more relaxed, confident, and successful person. Mastering the art of body language is just one of the ways to improve your image and build the rituals of success into your daily life. This 7 Minute Idea can make the difference between being great or just good at what you do.

Micro-Action: Sending Signals of Confidence

To be a leader, you must present yourself as a leader. You must walk like a leader, dress like a leader, feel like a leader, and talk like a leader. Some people are just born with these qualities, and others have to learn to strengthen these skills. If your actions form 55 percent of the world's opinion of you, rather than your words, how can you go about communicating confidence in everything you do? The answer lies in a series of these favorite micro-actions.

Micro-Action
· ·
Make an effective entrance.

The first micro-action you can use to help send the right message with your body language is to communicate confidence by making an effective entrance. We only have a few seconds to greet a client and make a first impression, so we need to be sure we use the time to let them know we are glad they are there and we are looking forward to this business. When I go out to greet a prospect or client, I step toward them quickly to show that I am excited to see them, look them in the eye, smile, and take their hand in a warm handshake. If I greet a customer I know well, I may actually hug them. I think the human touch is so important in cementing strong relationships, so I use my walk, my smile, and my first contact to communicate my confidence in the future of our strong business relationship.

When you enter a room, enter with a purpose, so people can see that you are glad to be there. Let the others in the room know that you appreciate their presence, too, and that you are ready to serve them with all the enthusiasm you have.

Micro-Action
. . . .
Stand up straight and walk proudly.

My second micro-action for communicating success with body language is to stand straight and walk tall. Note that I did not say you must *be* tall. I am five feet, three and one-half inches, and I have read all of the studies that say that tall men and women have an advantage in the business world. Look at the CEOs of America, many of them are well over six feet tall. Stature alone deems people more credible. While I cannot change my actual height, I know that my posture and stance can determine how tall others perceive me to be. Regardless your height, stand tall and walk tall. Incidentally, this advice is just as meaningful for those of you who are tall; whatever your height, let your straight posture speak volumes about your confidence in your abilities.

Micro-Action

. . . .

Be a strong presence.

Next, present yourself as a strong presence in any room or gathering. There are a number of small micro-actions, which if you use them as a matter of habit, will make this kind of presence second nature to you:

- *First—and always—maintain good eye contact with others in the room, and use your smile to put others at ease.* Positive eye contact and a warm smile can diffuse almost any difficult situation or set the tone for a positive meeting.

- *Next, position yourself well in important meetings.* Be sure that the principle players in the room have direct visual contact with you. If your meeting will take place at a long table, think before you sit. The head and foot of the table hold the most powerful positions; if you cannot occupy one of these positions, place yourself midway down one side of the table, so that the people at either end have direct visual contact with you. The weakest position of the table is immediately to the left or right of the head of the table. Of course, when offered a seat, you must sit there, but if you have the opportunity to choose your own location, choose it with these factors in mind.

- *Communicate with relaxed energy.* When I speak at a seminar or workshop, I deliver my message with lots of excitement. I think people can feed off any speaker's level of energy and engagement. When you are relaxed, engaged, and energetic, people feel that you are excited to be there, that you are listening to them, and that you are ready to help them in any possible way. When people sense your vitality and interest, they immediately listen more closely to you and respond more directly to your message.

- *Listen actively—and really listen.* You want to use all parts of your body to tell those around you that you are listening. Lean forward, watch the person who is speaking to you, and—if they tell you something important—repeat it back to them so they know that you understand their message.

- *Dress with respect for others in the room.* Do not misunderstand me, I am all for casual clothes, if casual is appropriate, but, in my business, casual *is not* appropriate. I am handling people's finances or counseling them on their path to success, and I think I need to look successful. Therefore, I wear a business suit to work every day. I like my doctor to wear a white coat and retail salespeople to wear recognizable uniforms so I can ask them for help. I also believe that clothes not only determine how others feel about you, but also how you feel about yourself. If you feel like a success, then you will *be* a success. What did you wear to the last important meeting you hosted? How will you be required to dress after your next promotion? If you really want that promotion, you should dress that way today. What we wear on the outside really does make us feel different on the inside.

Staying Connected through Networking

Regardless of what business you are in, I assume that you want your business to grow. Toward that end, here is another critical 7 Minute Idea:

· · · · ·

One of the most important ways you can make your business grow is through networking.

· · · · ·

Networking involves maintaining contact with a "network" of people in your industry and related businesses, social groups, and other organizations of shared interests for purposes beyond that of just socialization. I also call networking *community or organizational involvement.* Networking can help you grow your business in so many ways; it can improve your understanding of the marketplace, help you develop new customers, reveal new opportunities or technologies, and spread the word about new services or products.

In order to network effectively, you must first clarify exactly what you do and to whom you want to market your product or service. Your objectives must be clear if you want others to understand and help you achieve them. Then, you must be sure to communicate that information to all of your acquaintances and business associates, so that they understand precisely what you do and that you want to do business with them. It is also important to understand that networking is a two-way street. Often the best networking occurs when you find out what someone else's capabilities and services are, and you help them achieve their goals and dreams. Like most things in life, what goes around comes around. The more we help others grow their businesses, the more our own business grows.

Networking is an essential element of the rhythm of any successful businessperson's life. As you gain practice in networking, it becomes second nature to you. You develop a deeper understanding of your business and your customers, and you do not have to think twice about sharing that information with others.

Micro-Action: Describe Your Business

When I am teaching this material in a workshop, I will ask each participant, "Do you really know what you do?" Let that sink in for a minute. If you know you are in a business with hundreds of competitors who sell a product or service much like yours, in order to network effectively, you need to be able to describe yourself, your products, and your services in a way that clearly differentiates you from your competitors. Therefore, I will ask you the same question, "Do you really know what you do?" If you are going to network with other people, you must first have a clear understanding of what service or product you are offering to the market. Then you need to be able to explain what makes that service or product special.

In chapter 1, you learned the importance of differentiating yourself in the marketplace. You can build upon that information to develop a short and simple statement that explains clearly and simply what makes your business different from anything offered by your competitors. That is the first step in networking effectively.

You should be able tell your business associates and acquaintances what is unique about your product or service, what your objectives are for your business, and how they can help you reach those objectives. In our industry, this process of clarifying your objective is called *creating a unique positioning statement.* A unique positioning statement allows you, in one or two sentences, to say "Here is what I do and here is why that information might interest you."

As an example, I would say something like this: "I'm a financial advisor with a major New York brokerage firm. I run my business differently than most financial advisors. I would love to show you what I do." The response I usually get is something like this: "What do you mean you run your business differently?" That is my cue to deliver my unique positioning statement: I continue, "My mission is to educate, motivate, and encourage. I try to find out where my clients are today and where they want to be in the future, and then I create a comprehensive financial strategy to help take them there. Do you have a comprehensive financial strategy?"

In a few sentences, I say that the way I run my business is unique. Then I explain how my service differs from that of every other stockbroker or financial advisor. I want the listener to understand that he or she can benefit from doing business with me in ways that just are not possible with any of my competitors. Next, I simply tell them that I would like to show them what I do. I am using very nonthreatening language to let the listener know that I am willing to demonstrate just how good my services are.

To devise your own unique positioning statement, you first need to clarify in your own mind what you do, then boil it down to two or three sentences that clearly communicate how your business stands out. Then, you need to be able to speak those sentences easily and naturally. A simple micro-action can help you get started:

Micro-Action

. . . .

Take ten minutes right now to write a brief introduction statement that defines what you do and why you are different.

Your statement should be appropriate to your business, and it should really underscore the unique benefits you offer. Finally, it should be something that you can say as a matter of habit—short, simple sentences that just glide off the tip of your tongue. Write your statement here:

_____

_____

_____

_____

_____

_____

_____

_____

_____

_____

Resist the urge to try to describe yourself as the answer to everybody's every need. I see too many professionals who seem to want to be all things to all people. These people have not found their niche and, as a result, they cannot put into words the reason why someone should do business with them. Clearly and easily communicating your unique business strengths is one of the most important habits you can develop for growing your business.

Micro-Action: Describe Your Clients

Another 7 Minute Idea that can help you develop your networking skills:

· · · · ·

Being able to describe your business clearly is important, but it is equally important to be able to describe your clients.

· · · · ·

If you want those you network with to spread the word about what you do, it is critical that they know specifically to whom they should target that message. To make that happen, you need to be able to describe your ideal client clearly and easily. Just as introducing yourself appropriately should become a routine part of your business interactions, describing your customers clearly and simply can become a matter of habit for you with some thought and practice.

First, you must take the time to know your ideal client, customer, or prospect. Think a minute: Who are the most profitable clients in your current business, and what makes them profitable? What do they do for a living? What services do they buy from you? Why do they do business with you? Which clients do you enjoy working with the most? Of what types of clients would you like to have more?

As an example, as a financial advisor, here's how I would describe my ideal clients:

- Have significant investable assets

- Ages 40 to 85

- Incredibly nice to work with

- Reciprocating trust

- Have some understanding of how investments work, but are looking for a financial advisor to guide them in their financial decision making

- Build long-term friendships and tend to have long-term relationships

As you can see from their descriptions, an ideal client for me in my role as a financial advisor would have money to invest, be pleasant to work with, be seeking advice, and become long-term, loyal clients and friends.

The more you know about the customers and clients you want to develop, the better you will be able to describe them to your networking acquaintances. With that information, your networking contacts can help bring you into contact with the type of people you hope to serve.

I know that some of us are not sure about whom we want to attract to our businesses. Early in our careers, most of us are willing to take any clients. As our business matures, however, we know who we want to work for and with, and we are in a better position to target our efforts specifically toward those ideal clients. That is another important 7 Minute Idea that relates closely to the concept of choosing to be successful in your personal and professional life:

· · · · ·

You can build stronger skills and grow your business more effectively when you are able to concentrate your efforts on the tasks that best suit the business you want to have.

· · · · ·

Effective networking is an essential step in putting that idea into action.

To strengthen and develop the habit of being able to simply describe your ideal customer to your networking contacts, begin by taking a hard look at your current clients. Who are they? Where did they come from and what brought them to you? In most businesses, 80 percent of revenues comes from 20 percent of the clients. So, start with this micro-action:

Micro-Action

· ·

Draw up a list of the clients that provide the majority of your business and determine into what categories they fall.

These categories will be different for every business, of course. For my own financial investment business, for example, I categorized my clients by how they acquired their assets:

FIGURE 3.1

- Widows
- Inheritors
- 401(k) Rollovers
- Doctors and their spouses
- Entrepreneurs
- Pharmacists
- Other

If you are a homebuilder, you might categorize your best clients by what types of homes they build or where they build them. An advertising agency might categorize clients by the types of products or services they advertise, or the types of advertising media they use. Study the clients you have to understand more about the clients you want to attract to your business. When you are fully familiar with that information, you will be better able to tell your networking contacts specifically *who* you are hoping to serve in your business.

Micro-Action: Find New Networking Opportunities

In Jeff Gitomer's book, *The Sales Bible*, he describes what I refer to as his "fifty person rule," which dictates that if there are 50 people in a room at an event, Gitomer must be one of them. That is a great idea for networking. The more you are involved with the world around you, the better able you are to become a more active, vital, and successful part of that world.

That brings me to another great 7 Minute Idea:

· · · · ·

If you are trying to grow your business, you need to develop the habit of seeking out new networking opportunities.

· · · · ·

Keep an eye on the local newspaper; if there is an art gallery opening, a community meeting, or a charitable event that you want to go to and that is likely to attract people who could be good networking contacts, make sure you are one of the people in attendance at that event! Often these events are free, and they offer a great opportunity to introduce yourself to people who might be interested in your product or service.

Developing the habit of networking takes practice and a willingness to "stretch" your social skills. When you go to an event with the intention of networking, do not just stop to speak to one or two people. Introduce yourself to as many people as you can, and tell them what you do for a living as part of that introduction. As a micro-action:

Micro-Action
· ·
Find and attend one networking opportunity within the next two weeks, and introduce yourself to at least five people while you are there.

More than anything else, skillful networking is really just the habit of being involved in your community, meeting new people, and briefly and simply telling them the most important things you want them to know about you and your business. Remember, you are offering a unique advantage to the people who know and do business with you. With practice, networking becomes a routine part of your business and social world.

Moving to the Rhythm of Success

I hope that this chapter has helped you understand the importance of all of the small, routine things you do every day of your life. Many people believe that leading a successful life involves a monumental struggle up a steep hill. In fact, by changing the manner with which you approach some of the simplest things you do every day—the clothes you wear, the way you smile, how you introduce yourself to new acquaintances—you can build confidence both within yourself and among those you deal with every day.

Leading a successful life is, foremost, a matter of believing in your abilities; when you have that belief, you communicate it in everything you do. Remember, the people you meet will take away from their dealings with you more than just the words you speak. They will also read success in the way you dress, walk, speak, and carry yourself.

As I said earlier, our daily habits and rituals tell people who we are, but we define ourselves *to ourselves* by our dreams. By believing in our abilities, acknowledging our dreams, and letting go of the hundreds of negative messages we send ourselves each day, we are empowered by confidence and inner strength. Instead of letting the drumbeat of your negative illusions set the pace for your daily habits, I hope you will allow your dreams to build the strong and vibrant rhythm of a successful and well-lived life.

4

. . . .

Exceeding Your
Customers' Expectations

Almost every year on my birthday, my husband and I, with our two children, pack up the car and make the 80-mile trip to Memphis, Tennessee, to dine at Ruth's Chris Steak House. My husband makes the reservation in advance, and our arrival—as though eagerly anticipated—elicits a pleasant greeting at the front door. We are quickly shown to our linen-covered table in a dining room that is beautifully decorated, clean, and lovely—and it smells delicious. We sit and our menus arrive at the table with a tray of warm bread. I dutifully look over the menu (even though I already know what I will order) as we finish the bread in less than five minutes.

The servers work in teams, taking our order and delivering appetizers in almost no time. As I enjoy my first bite, I think,

"I can't believe I waited one whole year to taste this." From there it only gets better: The restaurant's homemade salad dressing is superb, and my steak is perfectly cooked and served sizzling on a hot plate. One of the waitstaff keeps my water glass full at all times, another quickly removes crumbs from the table, and the moment I look up for assistance, one of them is there to offer whatever I need. In other words, I am treated like the restaurant's most important diner whenever I visit. I look forward to this experience every year.

Many restaurants sell steak, but Ruth's Chris Steak House sells exceptional customer service. The company has chosen not to compete on price; instead, it invests in staff training and customer service, so that every diner will feel that *they* are the most important patron in that restaurant. Ruth's Chris' employees understand that their job is not to serve you a meal, but to provide you with a memorable experience.

What kind of experience are you providing to your customer? When someone comes into your automobile dealership, what are you prepared to give her for the $25,000 or $30,000 she will spend there? She can get a car anywhere, so what will you sell her that your competitor will not? When clients at my financial services firm write me a check for $500,000, I know that I am selling them more than just an investment portfolio and a monthly statement. I am selling my customers trust, confidence, and peace of mind. Everything I do, from the minute customers walk in my door and throughout our professional relationship, is designed to create a customer experience that supports those feelings.

Wouldn't it be great if all of our experiences as customers were like that? Wouldn't it be even better if we delivered as well thought-out and executed experiences to our own customers?

My primary purpose in writing this book is to help you become the best that you can be—to grow your business to a new peak of excellence, but what makes any business "the best"? The answer to that question is "Everything." Every aspect of our businesses—from the way we greet customers, to the quality and reliability of the product or service we provide, to the sincerity of our follow-up service—determines our success. In other words, "everything" can also be expressed as a single idea:

· · · · ·

Your business can reach the highest peak of excellence only if you commit to exceeding your customers' expectations.

· · · · ·

This chapter talks about 7 Minute Ideas and micro-actions that offer concrete steps toward achieving that goal.

Entering the Circle of Total Customer Experience

When you think of the term "customer service," what comes to your mind? Unfortunately, my thoughts drift immediately to poorly trained customer sales associates who are paid minimum wage to deliver minimum levels of service. The average sales associate simply cannot answer many service questions, so where do you turn for those answers? Most managers are unavailable or too busy to deal with the details of a sale, and who, in any of these organizations, exhibits any accountability for dealing with problems that you encounter *after* the sale?

Can you envision a world where customers receive respect and gratitude? Can you imagine a place where humans answer phone calls and messages receive prompt replies? How about a land where people take pride in knowing their products and in being able to solve your problems, rather than just "getting rid" of you as simply and inexpensively as possible? What if the sales clerk waiting on you actually knew how each product worked and could help you decide which would be your best choice? I am not describing some fairytale kingdom; I am describing a well-run business that offers customer service as it should be. I am describing a business that has carved out a niche for itself at the very peak of excellence within its marketplace. I am also describing a business that offers a *total customer experience.*

The truth is that most businesses seem more interested in building one-time sales, rather than long-term, satisfied customers. That is bad news for us as customers, but good news for us as businesspeople. In chapter 1, we discussed the following 7 Minute Idea:

· · · · ·

*Differentiating yourself can propel you
to unimagined success.*

· · · · ·

Here is another important and closely related 7 Minute Idea:

· · · · ·

*The total customer experience you offer differentiates
your business from that of your competitors.*

· · · · ·

Other people may sell the same products you sell or provide similar services, but only you can draw upon your own core strengths, beliefs, and energies to create a total customer experience specific to your business.

Building a Total Customer Experience

Margaret Stanzell is a friend of mine, who also happens to be a great trainer specializing in helping individuals and organizations improve their levels of customer service and accountability. She shared the following graph (Figure 4.1) with me ten years ago, and I still use it as part of my daily business model. I call this the circle of total customer experience.

The first ring in this graph, the core of any total customer experience, represents the basic products and services that a

FIGURE 4.1

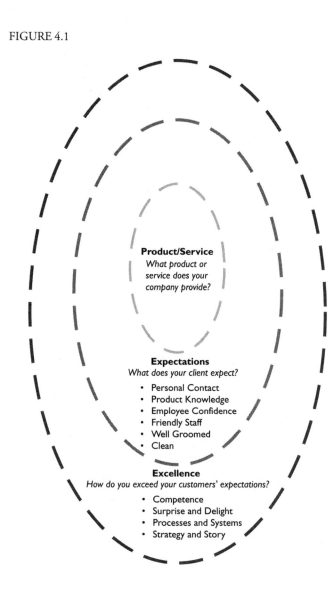

Product/Service
*What product or
service does your
company provide?*

Expectations
What does your client expect?

- Personal Contact
- Product Knowledge
- Employee Confidence
- Friendly Staff
- Well Groomed
- Clean

Excellence
How do you exceed your customers' expectations?

- Competence
- Surprise and Delight
- Processes and Systems
- Strategy and Story

business offers. The contents of this circle are rarely unique to your business; every automobile dealer sells some form of automobile, every financial advisor sells some form of investment products and services, every clothing manufacturer sells apparel. The quality of the items within this circle may vary from business to business, of course, and that quality certainly belongs at the heart of the total customer experience. Beyond that level of control, however, the contents of this inner circle do not differentiate one business from another of the same type.

The second circle of the chart represents the next layer of the total customer experience—your customers' expectations. Any customer doing business with you expects that you provide certain skills, qualities, and services; if you do not, you have failed to satisfy your customer and can expect to lose business. What does your client expect from the experience of doing business with you? I believe that most clients have very specific expectations of the companies with which they do business. Here, for example, are the things that I know my clients expect from my business:

- Personal contact

- Product knowledge

- Problem-solving abilities

- Friendly, pleasant, professional staff

- Clean offices

As you read that list, notice that the items listed there are essentially very basic qualities of a well-run business. That is not to say these qualities are commonplace; unfortunately, many businesses do not meet these basic customer expectations. On the other hand, you do not impress your customers simply by clearing the minimum threshold of their expectations; and you certainly do not set yourself apart from many of your competitors. In other words, the items within this second circle do not differentiate a company from its competition, and certainly do not provide any competitive advantage.

We cannot offer a total customer experience simply by working within the first two layers of this circle; we need to move into the third ring of the experience—Excellence. We cannot achieve excellence merely by not disappointing our customers in the process of offering them a basic product or service. Excellent service requires exceeding our customers' expectations. This outer ring of the circle—the largest and most influential component of your business's offering—includes the things that only *you* offer; the qualities, skills, and services that can dazzle your customers and differentiate your business from every competitor in your marketplace.

The contents of this circle represent your competitive advantage—and they represent the most creative, enjoyable, and demanding aspects of running your business. You will spend the rest of your career finding innovative ways to provide a total customer experience. The contents of this circle grow with your business and evolve in response to your customers' changing needs and preferences. The efforts you make to exceed your customers' expectations consistently make your business different tomorrow than it is today.

Micro-Action: Describe Three Things Only *You* Offer

Margaret Stanzell, who first shared these "circles" with me, is a great example of how the total customer experience works. My first invitation was to attend one of Margaret's training workshops (her product), which I assumed would be well prepared and include some useful ideas (my expectation). However, Margaret completely exceeded my expectations. Her workshop was thoughtful, funny, insightful, and packed with useful and helpful ideas geared perfectly to my needs. Even more than that, though, her energy filled the entire room. You left the training session feeling better about your whole life because you had spent a few moments with Margaret. Wow!

That is what you want your customer service experience to be like. When was the last time you personally had a total customer service experience? Do you recall when a salesperson listened to your needs and really delivered more than what he promised? Now, how are you planning to deliver your own total customer experience? It is time to dazzle your customers. To discover ways that you can exceed your customers' expectations, set aside your thoughts about your product or service and view your business from the perspective of your client. After you identify and understand your customers' primary expectations, then you can create strategies and solutions that go beyond those expectations. When your clients love it, you love it MORE! As each new abundantly satisfied customer walks away from your business, your sense of purpose is renewed.

I have to work hard to offer this kind of experience in my own business. Most of my new clients come to see me because a major event has occurred in their lives. In many cases, they have just received a large amount of money and the responsibility of investing it is overwhelming to them. They may have sold a business, retired from a company and received a 401(k) rollover, lost a loved one and received life insurance proceeds, or won a judgment and received a cash settlement. I can assure you that many of these clients are facing these once-in-a-lifetime decisions with some fear and trepidation. We hope to differentiate ourselves from our competitors by understanding our customers' fears and listening to their needs. Toward that goal, I offer my customers three things that they will not find at many of my competitors. These things are rooted in my purpose in life and in my core strengths and beliefs. They also combine to create a total customer experience:

1. *I offer my clients an education.* As you learned early in this book, I fulfill my purpose through growth and education. My emphasis on client education separates me from the crowd. It also makes the experience of dealing with each client much richer, more rewarding,

and more enjoyable for me, because they can more fully understand the products and services they are buying from me.

2. *More than just providing a service, I strive to give my clients dazzling service.* That commitment to excellence also sets me apart from my competitors. Rather than concentrating on one or two blockbuster efforts, I let my commitment to excellence guide me in all of the small details of the way I conduct my business. Later in this chapter, I will share some of my specific ideas for these details with you.

3. *When I deliver services to my customers, I deliver an entire experience—not just an isolated event.* You want clients to share an emotional connection with what they are learning from you. These emotional connections are built when we involve our senses—when we can see it, touch it, taste it, smell it, and hear it? What are your clients really experiencing? Are you willing to sit down and drink a cup of coffee with them? Do you look them squarely in the eye and firmly shake their hand? What kind of music is playing in your office or store? When I say that your client's time with you should be experiential, too, I'm saying that the way you conduct your business should create and maintain a feeling of trust, excitement, and loyalty within your customers.

What does your product or service really represent to the client that is buying it from you? Following on the next page is a micro-action that can help you determine that.

Micro-Action

. . . .

Take seven minutes right now to think of and record at least three things you offer your customers that none of your competitors provide.

Remember, these things must go beyond the basic product or service you offer, or the customers' minimum expectations. These three things represent what you are *really* selling to your customers, and knowing that is an important first step in knowing how to provide a complete customer experience.

Building Better Customer Service through Four Simple Ideas

Exceeding your customers' expectations can be a challenge; your customers will not come to you with a specific, written list of instructions on how to do it. You have to provide them with services and benefits they might not even realize they want or need when they begin their relationship with you. Despite the enormity of the task, most effective customer service ideas are not extravagant, expensive, or complicated. A combination of small, well-targeted efforts is usually the best way to create a blockbuster customer experience. Your total customer experience will convince your clients that dealing with you is unlike dealing with any other company in your field, and in the process, you will strengthen every aspect of your business.

Although each business must create its own unique blend of customer service, I believe four important concepts are the basis of any successful total customer experience:

1. Competence

2. Processes and Systems

3. Details

4. Strategy

Put these four concepts to work in forming your own total customer experience.

Being the Best—Competence

We've talked about the importance of constantly increasing your knowledge, building your skills, and expanding your experiences; no matter what business you are in, all of these qualities contribute to your competence. Remember this important 7 Minute Idea:

· · · · ·

*Your competence is the basis for any outstanding
customer service program you offer.*

· · · · ·

When your customers know that you know that you are providing them with exceptional customer service, you build both their respect and their loyalty. Outstanding reputations begin with a high level of competence.

Let me give you an example. In 1996, I was diagnosed with rheumatoid arthritis. Of course, I had excellent doctors in Arkansas, but due to some extenuating circumstances, my local doctors referred me to the Mayo Clinic in Rochester, Minnesota, for further review. The Mayo Clinic has an international reputation for excellent diagnostic services; my expectations were extremely high, based on that reputation.

When I arrived at the designated area for my scheduled appointment, I was directed to a huge open area filled with about 200 beige chairs that looked as though they had been in that waiting room since the 1960s. Although the waiting room was not luxurious, it made me feel that this clinic was all about serious business. I suspected that the Mayo Clinic invested its funds in top-quality medical staff and diagnostic equipment, rather than in its waiting-room furniture.

After four hours in that waiting room, it was finally my turn. The experience was well worth the wait—the treatment I received went beyond any experience I had ever had in a medical facility, and it certainly exceeded my expectations! The doctors worked as a team, and every member of the team spent time with me discussing my medical history. More importantly, their questions and close attention to my answers assured me that they cared deeply about fully understanding and solving my problem. Next, I went through a two-day series of tests. At the conclusion of those tests, the doctors had the answers they were looking for. They explained everything to me carefully and took more time to answer all of my questions. No rushing, no distracted grunts or mumbled responses to my comments and questions, no hurriedly scratched out prescription and a quick exit for these doctors. These specialists were experts in their field, and *my* issues were their greatest concerns during the time they spent with me. The magnificent medical minds of the Mayo Clinic staff and the extreme professionalism of the treatment they offered me combined to create an experience I will never forget.

This unparalleled level of competence has helped make the Mayo Clinic one of the most respected hospitals in the world. How competent are you in *your* chosen profession? Remember the 7 Minute Idea you learned in chapter 2: To grow professionally you must increase your knowledge. Here, I can add that:

· · · · ·

Your competence and your ability to model a successful customer service program, depends upon your professional growth.

· · · · ·

Have you created a plan for improving your professional knowledge and competence? Do your employees receive training and education about the products and services your company provides, and can they easily use it to answer customer questions or provide service? Customers are expensive to find and even more expensive to replace. The level of competence you demonstrate in your business plays an important role in delivering a total customer experience—and in building long-term customer loyalty.

Providing Reliability—Process and Systems

If you want consistently excellent customer service throughout your company, then you must develop a process for delivering that service. A thorough employee-training program is part of that process. Standardize all employee procedures—the proper way to deal with a client, wait on a customer, answer the phone, or record a sale. Your systems and processes prepare employees to greet people entering your business, answer their questions, and resolve their problems. Customers should receive the same high level of professional service *every time* they interact with *anyone* associated with your business.

The first step in honing your processes is to make sure that all employees are fully trained and confident in their knowledge of their job. Your customers should not be left waiting while an employee scurries around trying to find someone to answer a question about a basic transaction or issue. Training processes should cover all of the tasks employees participate in, from answering the phone to attending client luncheons. If you need help designing a training process for your business, contact your local chamber of commerce and ask for the name of someone in your area who can assist you. By investing in thorough employee training up front, you save customers' time, reduce their frustration, and contribute to a better customer experience.

The speed and convenience of the processes also contribute to the reliability of your service. We live in a microwave age. Building speedy service into your systems demonstrates respect for your customers' busy schedules. I encourage you to develop processes that emphasize customer convenience, including proper preparation and planning, easy access parking, automated checkout—anything that can make your customer's experience smoother, faster, and more trouble-free.

Paying Attention to Details—Surprise and Delight

Exceeding customer expectations means surprising and delighting your customers, and that happens when you pay close attention to the details of your business operation. Everyone loves a surprise. Do you remember when your husband sent you flowers for no reason at all and the handwritten note seared your heart, or the surprise birthday party your parents threw for you when you were ten years old? Our clients are surprised and delighted by the attention we pay to even the smallest details of our business transactions.

Micro-Action: Create an Exceptional Customer Experience

Every business has unique opportunities for providing surprising and delightful customer service, but here are just a few small details—micro-actions—that can make a big difference in your customers' experience:

- *Give your client a warm greeting.* A client's first impression forms within the first few seconds of meeting you, so the way you greet your customers is incredibly important. I make it a habit to greet people quickly and graciously when they enter my office. Your greeting should tell customers that you are grateful they have chosen to come to you and that you are anxious to help them in any way you can.

- *Focus fully on your customer.* When you are serving a customer or client, you must fully focus all of your attention on that person. I want to make sure that when I am working with a client, I am *fully* in their presence. That means that I am listening to them, my phone is turned off and messages sent to voice mail, and I am not reading or responding to e-mail.

- *Take time to explain your product or service.* Take time with your customers to educate them about the product or service you offer. Do not rush them to make a decision. Remember, developing a relationship with your customer is more than simply making a sale. Developing a strong customer relationship is an essential element of providing a total customer experience.

- *Pay attention to the appearance of your business and its staff.* Everyone who works in your place of business should look like the ideal company representative: clean, neat, and eager to serve. If you own a retail business, make sure your employees wear some kind of uniform or badge so that customers can easily spot someone who can answer their questions or concerns. The building's appearance is important, too. All interiors should be immaculately clean and tasteful. The customer should begin to be drawn to your business before even entering the building; flower urns, greenery, and other outdoor decorations show customers that you care about making their experience with you as pleasant as possible. Clean restrooms, a vase of flowers on the reception desk, magazines in the lobby—these are the small details that can make a monumental difference in the way your customers perceive your business.

- *Create a pleasant working atmosphere.* I cannot tell you how important it is to make your business a fun place to work. There is nothing that contributes more to a positive customer experience than a business staffed by people who are glad to be there. Customers can sense this the minute they walk in your door—they can even sense it over the telephone! Again, small details create this kind of atmosphere; for example, soft, appropriate music, good lighting, clean employee lounges or break rooms all make employees feel happier and more valuable. Those feelings contribute to improved performance, productivity, and sales—and better service for your customers.

- *Demonstrate a commitment to community service.* I believe that giving back to the community that helps pay your bills is one of the most important benefits you can offer your customers. I encourage you to participate in fundraisers, help collect and contribute to emergency funds, offer to match employee contributions, and let the community know that it can count on your support. Your willingness to invest money, time, and effort into improving your community improves the community's trust in and appreciation for your business.

Promoting Your Company's Image—Strategy and Story

I believe that all companies need a strong identity—a strategy and story employees can wrap their arms around that the public cannot fail to notice. All businesses must have new customers to grow, and a strong company identity and image is what attracts new customers. A company's image is the face it shows to the world, therefore image is a critical part of a strong and memorable customer experience. Here is an important 7 Minute Idea for you to remember about your company's image:

· · · · ·

The small details that differentiate your business from others form the highlights of your company's image.

· · · · ·

To understand the importance of this idea, look at the following image:

FIGURE 4.2

What do you see: an aerial photograph of Jonesboro, Arkansas, a partial picture of the moon? This picture is simply a collection of dark areas with no discernable highlights, making it hard to draw any concrete conclusions about what it represents. However, when I highlight the important areas of the image, as in Figure 4.3 on the next page, you can clearly see that this is actually the picture of a cow:

FIGURE 4.3

This is a simple visual shift, but it does an excellent job of illustrating the importance of emphasizing the details of your customer service to present a strong and identifiable image of your business to the public. So many companies are just cookie-cutter versions of every other similar business; they have no special features, no niche, no story to tell their employees and customers. You do not want a grey and "faceless" business. You want your business to be immediately recognizable and very memorable.

Micro-Action: Ask Your Clients for Feedback

If your corporate image is not even clear to you, here is a micro-action that can help you clarify that image right now:

Micro-Action

. . . .

Contact five of your top clients, and ask them what they like best—and least—about the service you are performing for them.

Their answers should tell you a great deal about your corporate image. Do your clients see you as a reliable source for information, products, or expertise? Do they enjoy the personal attention you offer them? Do they appreciate the fast turnaround you offer or your willingness to set and meet aggressive deadlines? Do they really turn to you only because your prices are low? Do they view you as a "stop-gap" or last-minute choice, rather than a professional solution? If multiple clients offer similar responses, those similarities are the highlights that form your image, and that image tells the story that your employees and clients will understand about your business.

In a typical grocery store, placed right at eye level in very conspicuous locations throughout the store, are items that people *want* rather than *need.* It is called "shelf space." That is a strategy for selling impulse items—and it works. Constructing a strong image is a powerful strategy you can use to catch the attention of your customers. You want to make sure that your strengths are clear and easy to identify, so that your customers immediately recognize your image and remember it long after they leave your office or store. You want to create "shelf space."

Your customers begin forming their opinion of your business from the moment they pull into the parking lot. A million small details contribute to that image and the total customer experience. Is your image what you want it to be? If it is, work to strengthen it. If it is not, now is the time to start changing it.

Making the Most of Face-to-Face Contact

I make many presentations, both as a professional speaker and in meetings with clients who come to me for financial advice. Although I may spend more time before the public than most, no matter what your profession, you probably spend some portion of your workweek making presentations or working one-on-one with clients or customers. Whether you are delivering a sales presentation, explaining a contract to a new client, conducting a doctor/patient interview, delivering a report to your team, helping a customer choose a pair of shoes, or holding a one-on-one meeting with your supervisor, your ability to perform well in face-to-face meetings is important to your overall professional success.

Each time you engage in any kind of face-to-face contact with clients or co-workers, you have a small window of time in which to deliver your most important pieces of information. Making the most of that time is one way that you can contribute to your clients' positive experience. You want the people to leave your meetings feeling better informed and energized about the topics you covered. Delivering face-to-face information effectively and engagingly shows respect for your listeners and contributes to the quality of their experience with you and your business.

Remember the seven minute rule you learned early in this book. Most people will stop listening to what you say after seven minutes. Think about it for a minute (you will not need seven minutes, this time). Most of us spend a lot of time watching television, and most television programs deliver information to us in small seven minute chunks. A commercial comes on at the end of each period, so we stop paying attention, go to the bathroom or kitchen, and then snap back for another short period of attentive listening. Technology has trained us to have a limited attention span.

Few of us can wrap up everything we need to say in seven minutes, however, so we have to find ways of delivering information in manageable "chunks," and recalling the wandering attention of our listeners. Instead of trying to force your listener's brain to do more than it can do, you can use a few simple tools to help break your presentation or meeting into manageable seven minute segments. If you implement these tools, your listeners will learn more, remember more, and walk away feeling better about the meeting and your services.

I use these strategies, and that is one of the reasons I am known as The 7 Minute Coach™. I work within the parameters of what people can handle. The seminar classes I teach can last anywhere from four hours to eight hours, but I break each of these classes down into seven minute segments. I also use some specific tools for capturing and holding my audience's attention. No matter what profession you are in, you can use the actions I describe in the following sections to keep and hold your listener's attention.

Micro-Action: Capture the Listener's Attention with Verbal Flags

Every presentation, appointment, consultation, or retail sales encounter contains a few specific points that listeners must remember. Here is an important micro-action to remember:

Micro-Action

. . . .

Highlight important points for your listeners by using verbal flagging statements.

These statements give your listeners a "heads-up," so they understand that you want them to pay special attention to the next piece of information.

I have found that one of the most effective verbal flagging techniques is to lower your voice, and pause. Immediately you will have their attention. Another effective way to be sure your listeners are not on a mental vacation when you are delivering an important point is to flag their attention by saying, "This is one of the key points of our discussion." Here are other effective verbal flags:

- "Here is something you may want to remember."

- "You may really want to listen to this."

- "Are you ready?"

Teachers have used these kinds of flagging statements for years, and you probably remember some of them from your past. When you see your listeners headed toward a mental vacation, use a verbal flagging statement to snap them back. Consider it your way of saying to them, "I may only have you for the next seven minutes, but those seven minutes are mine!"

Micro-Action: Engage Listeners with Call-to-Action Statements

Another important micro-action for engaging your listeners is this:

Micro-Action

. . . .

Use call-to-action statements to involve your listeners and engage their attention.

Listening can become a very passive experience; your listeners will get more from your presentation if they are actively engaged

in its information. Asking them to perform some action or contribute opinions involves your listeners in the presentation
process, helps break up the information, and emphasizes important points you want them to remember.

Handouts, such as a simple printed agenda with room for
jotting down meeting notes, are a great help in delivering call-
to-action statements. I often prepare small, informational handouts, whether I am delivering a seminar or just conducting a
personal appointment with a client. Then, I use the handouts to
help call listeners to action by saying:

- "You may want to write this on your piece of paper."

- "You may want to write this in your book."

- "Put a star by this piece of information."

- "Circle this."

- "Underline this."

When you use a call-to-action statement like these it gives
your listener a chance to participate.

Surveying the people that you are talking to is another way
to issue a call to action. Ask questions to be sure that they are
with you, to gather their response to the information you are
delivering, to find out how the topic you are speaking about affects them personally, and to engage them actively in the presentation. If your listener's attention is about to drift away from

the topic at hand, any specific request for action on their part will bring them back—for another seven minutes or so!

Micro-Action: Use Visual Effects to Drive Home Ideas

I also recommend that you *use visual effects, even in simple one-on-one appointments, to help illustrate points.* Do you remember the picture of the cow? I used that visual effect to help drive home an important point about our perception of images. I am also a children's magician by hobby, so when I am doing a live presentation for 400 people, I pull out a newspaper and begin tearing it into little strips as I tell a story that illustrates an important point; then, bam! The newspaper is magically back together again, and for seven more minutes, the audience is back with me.

Engaging your listeners visually does not require you to be a magician. Photographs, charts, graphs, PowerPoint presentations, drawing on a dry-erase board, product samples—whatever your product, process, or service, you can find some visual aid that can help you present your material memorably to your readers. Whenever you present a visual effect, you momentarily surprise your listeners and help call their attention back to the discussion. Visual effects also work as a memory aid for your listeners, to help them understand and remember important information within your presentation.

Micro-Action: Increase Your Listener's Understanding with Personal Stories

Another micro-action for improving face-to-face contact is this:

Micro-Action

. . . .

Use personal stories and anecdotes to illustrate your information, provide "breaks" in your presentation, and to recall the attention of your listeners.

People generally do not recall endless streams of facts; but when memorable stories explain those facts, the stories stay with listeners for a long time.

Take a story I use often in my presentations on investing and that I wrote about in my first book, *The Million Dollar Car and $250,000 Pizza*. I love to tell people that if they make an agreement with themselves to put the same amount of money into their retirement plan that they are willing to spend on their car payment and pizza, they could save over a million dollars by the time they retire. To illustrate this point, I tell them that, if their car payment was $340, and if at age 30 they would commit to saving that amount each month, by the time they are 65, their savings, assuming a 9 percent return, would have grown to a million dollars. Next, I tell them that the average family spends about $25 when they go out for pizza. I then ask them, what if you quit taking your family out for pizza once a week, and instead, invested the money in any mutual fund investment that has averaged at least 9 percent? Again, if they start that process at age 30, by the time they reach age 65 they would have accumulated an additional $250,000. So I tell my listeners, for the price of a monthly car payment and a weekly night out for pizza, you can retire as a millionaire.

This is a very simple illustration, but I can tell you that it is one of the most effective and memorable moments of my presentation for some people. It helps them truly understand the power of relatively simple decisions and, at the same time, it helps bring back the attention of any of my listeners who have begun to mentally drift away from my presentation. I cannot tell you how often I run into people who have heard one of my presentations in the past and they say "Hey, I remember you! You're the 'pizza lady.'" Tell stories. It helps people understand your message and it brings them back from their mental vacations.

Using Micro-Actions to Exceed Customer Expectations

Here is a final 7 Minute Idea for this chapter:

· · · · ·

The future of your company's success lies in your customers' opinions about you and your business.

· · · · ·

This idea is one more illustration of how you make the biggest leap toward positive growth and development by paying attention to the smallest details of your operation. The brilliance of your board of directors or the fabulous new cost-saving strategy you just implemented do not guarantee your success. Your success is more likely to come from a single customer walking away from your business feeling satisfied, important, and overwhelmed by the quality of the service he just received. If you can exceed one customer's expectations, you can do it for another and then another, and soon your customers will become your best advocates.

As I said, your customer service differentiates you from your competition, and in that regard, your techniques will be your own. Let me finish this chapter, though, by sharing some simple micro-actions that will help you exceed your customers' expectations and contribute to creating a total customer experience for your business:

- *Ask your clients about their interests and hobbies, and then mail them notices about attractions or information related to those interests.*

- *Send your clients a few of your favorite recipes.* This simple act shares a part of your personality with your clients and can establish an even stronger sensory bond with them.

- *Send birthday cards to your clients, their children, grand-children, or pets.*

- *Send anniversary cards on the date they first became your client.*

- *Greet or make personal contact with clients who visit your business, even if your staff is attending to their needs.*

- *Host a one-on-one networking appointment with clients.* Allow them to become a part of your team.

- *Put fresh flowers out in front of your business or in your reception area.*

- *Send pictures of your team or employees to your best clients so they know what you look like.*

- *Constantly tell your clients how much you appreciate their business.* Handwritten thank-you notes are one example.

- *Stop taking your clients out to eat.* Instead, invite your clients to have lunch with you at your office. It can be a meal as simple as spaghetti and a salad. The key is to involve your clients' senses. When they can smell the delicious aroma and taste the delicious foods, those pleasurable thoughts will be linked with you and your office.

Adding such small efforts to the outer ring of your Circle of Total Customer Experience should be a process that lasts throughout your professional career. Never stop asking how you can better position your company, create more efficient processes, or make your clients happier with the services you offer. Customer service is so much more than lip service; it must become a focal point of your company if you plan to survive. Remember:

· · · · ·

The total customer experience you offer differentiates your business from that of your competitors.

· · · · ·

I have heard it said that if a person has one negative experience, they will tell 20 people, but if they do not have a problem, they may never tell a soul. I believe that saying is true; if you do not mess up, your customers probably will not complain. However, silence from your customers does not help your businesses grow. If you exceed your customers' expectations, you build a strong and ongoing network of consumer support for your business. Through delivering consistently dazzling total customer experiences, you give your clients a real reason to tell all of their friends, family members, and co-workers about what makes you different and why they recommend that others should do business with you. The power of providing a total customer experience can feed an ongoing process of growth and change in your company and in every aspect of your professional life.

5

. . . .

Powering Growth through Momentum

Don't you love those wonderful days when you wake up before your alarm clock goes off, your hair looks just right, you hit all the green lights on the way to work, you have a great day planned, and with every minute that passes things just keep getting better and better? Every "yes!" moment of your splendid morning feeds your optimism and boosts your energy, so soon you are flying through the day, jumping hurdles, solving problems, and tackling new projects—you are on a roll!

That expression perfectly describes the power of momentum. A rock dislodged from the top of a hill will begin to roll downward. At first, it moves slowly and without much power; any small dip or rise in the path could stop it and you would need to push it again to get it moving. Once that rock builds momentum, though—once the mass of that rock is fully in motion—it gains strength and speed; it hops and bounces over larger and larger obstacles, until nothing can stand in its way or stop its progress. That's the same kind of power you develop on those perfect mornings when everything falls into place; every success builds your momentum until it seems that *nothing* can stop you. That is the power of momentum.

Jim Collins, in his book *Good to Great,* uses the analogy of a flywheel to describe the way a business can use momentum to power ongoing growth and development, and I think that is a great analogy. A flywheel is a heavy disk; when you push the flywheel to put it into motion, its weight makes it spin faster and faster. As it spins, it builds and stores energy. The longer the flywheel keeps spinning, the faster it goes, and the more energy it produces. That energy can be used to power anything from a car engine to a potter's wheel. In Collins's analogy, the same process powers the growth of business. In the beginning, you need to push hard and persistently to set the flywheel of growth in motion. Then each small, positive act contributes to a small change in position. Those small changes build and the wheel of growth spins faster and faster; finally, the momentum of that movement becomes a force all on its own. When you power your business by momentum, you need less brute strength to keep the "wheel" turning, and can instead focus your energy on supplying targeted, consistent, and well-planned boosts.

As Collins points out, though, getting the wheel started takes persistence. The first few efforts you make will be the most difficult, and they might not seem to make much difference in your position. Think about pedaling a bicycle; you start out slowly, straining against the pedals, wobbling along the path. You cannot concentrate fully on the road ahead, because you are exerting all of your energy in getting started. Every time you push the pedals, however, it gets a little bit easier. You build momentum, and that momentum helps you get more forward movement out of less muscle power. The force of your momentum straightens your bike, helps power it along, and gives you the freedom to concentrate on guiding it in the right direction.

I talk a lot in this book about the power of small changes. That power lies in momentum. Once you set the wheels of change moving in your personal life or in your business, you begin powering the process of growth. Your momentum speeds you through the challenges of daily business life and even helps you overcome those large obstacles that periodically appear in your path.

The process of powering growth through momentum involves five stages:

1.   Identifying your starting point

2. Aligning your energies with your life's purpose and passion to begin the process of change

3. Drawing upon your strengths to create a strategy that will shape your identity

4. Creating systems to regularly feed growth

5. Keeping your growth on track toward long-term goals

This chapter talks a bit about each of these stages, and I share with you some of my own experiences in starting and keeping the flywheel of growth in motion. I will also tell you about my firsthand experience at helping to plan and execute important changes within my own business. I learned some valuable techniques for building momentum through change, and the information you learn here will allow you to apply those same techniques to your own process of personal and professional growth.

Determining Your Starting Point

As a financial advisor, the years 1999 through 2002 were extremely difficult. As you may recall, the S&P 500 fell from 1,553 in March of 2000 to 768 in October of 2002, in a market decline of approximately 50 percent. That 2½ year period seemed like a bad dream that never ended. I had been through plenty of other market declines and fully understood the underlying risk in the stock market; financial advisors and investors alike know that volatility is part of the industry. But, I assure you, living through those 31 months tested me to the core.

One of the great lessons in life is that it is the difficult times that strengthen us. They center us and help make us aware of what is really important in life. And, they can force us to stop and re-evaluate everything in our lives. At that difficult time I realized that I needed to create a plan for building momentum in my professional life. The first step in formulating a road map for that plan was to fully understand my current situation.

As I began to re-evaluate my life, I first looked to my *purpose*. If growing and helping others grow was truly the primary purpose of my life, then that must be my starting point. I needed to take my eyes off of the circumstances surrounding me and focus my attention on remaining true to my purpose. To gain momentum in my business life, I decided to grow in four main areas:

1. *Education.* I wanted to read, and study and attend conferences to continue to increase my understanding of my profession.

2. *Productivity.* I wanted to improve my understanding of technology.

3.   *Organization.* I wanted to de-clutter my work envi-
     ronment and create a system of filing and paper man-
     agement designed to make my life more efficient.

4.   *Processes and Systems.* I wanted to implement repeatable
     processes and systems to increase client satisfaction.

Each of us are in radically different places in life. Some of
you may find yourselves struggling to recover from setbacks
such as those I faced between March of 2000 and October of
2002 or, like Ernest Shackleton and his men, you may find
yourself trapped by life's difficult circumstances. Wherever you
are, if you want to regain momentum in your life, you must decide to move forward. You must take the first step.

That leads me to a 7 Minute Idea:

· · · · ·

*To begin moving toward meaningful change, you must
clearly understand your starting point.*

· · · · ·

Do you know where you are today and in what direction
your current efforts are taking you? Are you in control of your
movement in that direction or do you feel that your daily
progress is being determined by things or circumstances beyond
your control? To set the wheel of growth in motion down the
path you want to follow, you need to understand what is sweeping you along your current trajectory.

Micro-Action: Describe Your Starting Point

Here is a simple micro-action that can help you determine where you are today, where you are heading, and why you are heading in that direction:

Micro-Action

. . . .

Ask yourself the following questions. Then, in the lined space that follows this list, describe your current position and the forces that influence it. Be very honest with yourself as you answer these questions:

- Does your job allow you to utilize your gifts and talents fully?

- Are you able to share your strengths in your current workplace?

- Is your income appropriate for the level of service you are providing to your clients?

- Are there circumstances beyond your control that have caused problems in your current job?

- Is a lack of skill preventing you from moving forward in your company? What are those skills and when can you begin learning them?

- Are you really in the right career?

Describe your starting point:

_____
_____
_____
_____
_____
_____
_____
_____
_____
_____
_____

Putting the Wheel in Motion

There is a big difference between talking about momentum and actually getting up from your desk and taking specific actions to allow momentum to happen in your life. After 31 months of declining stock markets, and declining momentum, there came a point where I could simply accept the circumstances occurring around me, over which I had no control, or I could decide to take action. I believed taking action would be the better choice.

After recognizing my starting point, I was ready to put the wheel of change in motion; to do that successfully, I needed to align my work with my life's purpose, passion, and strengths.

The only way any of us can truly excel in our personal and professional lives is to build upon our strengths. In other words, if you want to achieve your personal best, you must give yourself permission to *do what you do well.*

Begin asking yourself these questions: What do I love doing most at work? Where am I most competent? What activities bring me the most fulfillment? Of course, the answer will be, "I love to work on the projects that most closely align with my life's purpose, passion, and strengths."

Remember this 7 Minute Idea:

· · · · ·

When you align your work with your life's purpose, passion, and strengths, you find that work changes from something you are paid to do to something you are called to do.

· · · · ·

You become more productive, more fulfilled, and more excited by the work you do. We all have unique gifts and talents. Take just five minutes now to think about yours. Are you:

- good in math?

- a problem solver?

- a peacemaker?

- a comforter?

- a good listener?

- a leader?

- an encourager?

- a motivator?

- a teacher?

- an administrator?

- a manager?

Micro-Action: Align Your Purpose, Passion, and Strengths

In chapter 1, you explored your purpose and passions in life. To help you put those understandings to work in determining how to get the strongest start on building the momentum of your own personal or professional growth, here is another micro-action:

Micro-Action

. . . .

In the next seven minutes, write the answer to this question in the space on page 139:

How can you align your actions (at work or at home) with your purpose, passion, and strengths to make changes that will put the flywheel of growth in motion within your life?

_____
_____
_____
_____
_____
_____
_____
_____
_____
_____
_____

Building Momentum through Strategy and Story

Two things separate you from your competition: a very specific strategy for your business and a story that tells the community you live in—or even the world—why you are different. Your strategy needs to be specific, compelling, and easily communicated. Every manager, employee, and client should understand it. Whether you are a financial advisor, an accountant, a plumber, or a doctor, you need a clear and powerful strategy and a compelling story to differentiate you from your competition and attract new clients. Strategy and story are essential for powering the momentum of any business. Strategies are important to management teams. Stories are important to your customers. Creating and sharing your story can transform your business overnight. What is your strategy?

Is it simple and succinct enough that you can easily explain it to a prospective client in your first meeting? What price are you willing to pay to raise the bar on your own personal competence so that people will come to you as an expert and choose you over all other service providers in your field?

Consider the strategy of Federal Express. Delivery services have been around since the Pony Express. Nevertheless, Fred Smith, the founder of Federal Express, developed a concept for a service that would guarantee overnight delivery anywhere in the United States. How different is that? Who would have thought you could develop a system of trucks and planes to take a package from Jonesboro, Arkansas, to New York City in one day? Smith did not stop there, though, he also wrapped his strategy in a story; "Absolutely, positively overnight." Smith believed in the strategy, told a compelling story, and today Fed Ex boasts revenues in excess of $29 billion.

Stories build dreams. They create hope in both the senior executives and the people to which they sell. Most corporations have some sort of corporate strategy, but very few have stories. Consider, for example, Chico's FAS, a clothing company started in 1983 by Marvin and Helene Grainick. Chico's is a great example of a company with a compelling story, based on a very different (there is that word again, *different*) sales strategy. The Chico's story is that they deliver great-looking, comfortable, high-quality clothing, in a friendly, helpful environment, at a great price. Everything about Chico's strategy tells their story. The company designs many of their own fabrics, using bright, interesting colors. Chico's created its own size structure: 0, 1, 2, and 3; not the standard 8, 10, 12, 14 that women in this country are accustomed to. Chico's clothes are great for travel and the company produces some original pieces that they sell year after year, which allows you to build your Chico's wardrobe, add to your collection, and mix and match. Its small boutiques are in great locations and have a warm, inviting atmosphere. The sales staff is friendly and helpful, and they really try to assist you in putting together clothes that fit your shape, style—and budget. Chico's offers frequent sales and the company sends out coupons to its regular customers; the clothes last for years and move well from season to season. Wearing Chico's clothes makes me feel good. I am hooked on the Chico's story of great style, great value, and great service.

Strategies and stories are critically important factors for any individual or organization that wants to be different tomorrow. Many corporations invest millions of dollars in advertising, to help tell their story to the world, but the most effective stories do not come from marketing teams. They spring from successful strategies that help clearly differentiate one business from its competitors. When you have a sound and strong business strategy, you do not need to tell your clients who you are or what you do—your unmistakable identity explains that for you. Then, your story will explode from the mouths of your exceedingly satisfied customers. Starbucks does not have to tell you why you are paying $3 or more for a cup of coffee. You know from the moment you walk in the door that you are paying for the experience of having a great cup of coffee from a hip company with modern sensibilities and a social conscience. That is Starbucks' strategy at work. Federal Express does not just sell a delivery service. They sell you a time guarantee; their strategy was to build a business by guaranteeing next day, on-time delivery. Today, the company's name is synonymous with that strategic guarantee. Chico's does not have to rave about its great service; its stores, products, staff, and customers tell that story clearly and compellingly.

Remember this 7 Minute Idea:

· · · · ·

A strong strategy and story provide ongoing energy to feed the power of growth and change in your personal and business lives.

· · · · ·

Creating a strategy and a story is one of the most important points in this book. There is no value you can put on "word of mouth" marketing. Your strategy and your story allow your customers to become part of your best advertising.

Micro-Action: Frame Your Strategy

If you want to be different, you must create a strategy that makes that difference scream out its story in the marketplace. A micro-action that does this:

Micro-Action
· ·
Take ten minutes to identify three concepts you view as your competitive advantages—aspects of your strategy that differentiate you within your workplace or your business within its marketplace:

1. _____
   _____

2. _____
   _____

3. _____
   _____

Micro-Action: Create Your Story

Once you have clarified your competitive advantages, you want to develop or refine your strengths into a compelling story—an easily understandable story, embraceable by your employees and your customers. For the next micro-action:

Micro-Action
· ·
Take ten minutes to describe your story on the following page:

_____

_____

_____

_____

_____

_____

_____

_____

_____

_____

_____

Maintaining Momentum with Systems

With our strategy and story in place, my team began powering the wheel of change in our business. Next, we turned our attention to finding a system that built and fed the momentum of our growth. We did not want to have to come into the office each morning and reinvent the wheel; we needed systems that would help us keep basic processes on track and allow us to focus our creative energies on other aspects of our business. Strategy and story begin the process of growth; systems build and maintain its momentum.

To systematize our strategic processes, we began fully implementing a contact and customer management program called ACT! ACT! is a database/contact management system that allows us to manage our daily client contacts and keep track of our ongoing customer commitments. The program prints out a daily activity sheet containing specific information about the tasks we have planned for that day. Using ACT!, I know who I need to telephone, how many appointments I need to host, how many personal contacts I need to make, and how many proposals I need to send out—every day.

We also put forms into place. We created client agendas so that when we sat down with our clients, we would know what we wanted to speak to them about. We created detailed client budget sheets and client contact records, so that after we met or spoke with a client, we could keep detailed notes on every conversation. By transferring those notes into ACT!, we maintain a detailed record of every moment of our history with each client.

To get the most powerful boost from the systems we put in place, we worked to become experts in implementing ACT! and making it work for our business. We hired consultants to come in and teach us how to use it. We bought books on it. We experimented with creating personalized reports. We downloaded it onto our personal PDAs. We were dangerously close to becoming "technology geeks"! The time and effort has paid off many times over. Contact management software is now a basic tool of our company, and all of us are masters at using it.

Using some simple forms, procedures, and contact management software helps everyone in our company stay on top of the processes necessary to put our strategy into action. This system helps us live up to our unique identity and "do what we say we will do." To keep any strategy alive and in action, you must find appropriate systems to manage essential processes. Remember this important 7 Minute Idea:

· · · · ·

Systematizing the processes necessary to support your strategy lets you focus your energies on growth, rather than maintenance.

· · · · ·

Two years ago, with our strategy, story, and systems in place, we began pushing the flywheel of growth at my company. We lived by our five-point strategy, and used it to help educate our clients and grow their assets. As a result, our clients and prospects fully understood the benefits of working with our company—they heard our story loud and clear. We used our systems to manage the processes necessary to support our strategy. The flywheel of change in our organization quickly gained incredible momentum. After educating our clients, putting our strategy into action, and implementing a system to support that strategy, our business grew by 67 percent in 2004.

Micro-Action: Identify Systems and Processes

What positive steps can you take to develop the strategy, story, and systems that help power the forces of change in your business? Here is a micro-action to help:

Micro-Action

. . . .

Take five minutes now to explore the answers to these questions:

- Have you found systems that can keep building the momentum of your change?

- Is your employee training implemented in a systematic fashion so all of your employees feel equipped to do their jobs? Could you have a new hire up and running within a month?

- Do you have a process for thanking a new customer for doing business with you?

- Are all of your daily tasks necessary? What simple forms and procedures could you put in place to streamline processes and reduce the costs of maintaining them?

You learn more about reviewing and updating your systems in the next chapter of this book. Check the Appendix of this book for sample forms and other ideas to streamline your business through processes and systems.

Steering the Forces of Growth toward Long-Term Goals

Momentum fuels the engine of change, but even the most powerful engine needs periodic adjustment. Just as momentum can propel you to the peak of excellence, if your business goes off course, the power of momentum can quickly take you where you do not want to go. Consider that bicycle journey we spoke of earlier. The faster your bike speeds along, the more carefully you have to guide it and the further you need to look down the road ahead. Obstacles can loom up quickly, and it is easy to speed through turns without really being sure where they are taking you. Like any force, you must manage momentum. Our systems will keep fueling our development, but periodically we need to step back and re-examine the way our business is changing and developing, to determine whether we are still moving in the right directions.

Forming Sustaining Partnerships

One way to sustain our momentum and keep it on track is to create a strong network of professional advisors who can continually refresh and develop our perspective on our approach, processes, and attitudes. I recommend that everyone find and make full use of mentors as a tool for improving competence in both general and industry-specific practices. By drawing upon the support, experience, and ideas of a number of mentors, advisors, coaches, partners, and friends, you can help feed and sustain the momentum of your personal *and* professional growth.

I work with a number of partners, and the first among these is my spouse, Mark Lewis. We make a great team. He is an instructor of law at Arkansas State University. His gift is teaching and he is incredibly talented. He also is a fantastic husband and father. Mark and I are a team. We are partners.

My parents, Ann and Al White of Pine Bluff, Arkansas, have been important mentors and partners in my life, as are my friends and my team members at my work. The many teachers I have had the benefit of working with throughout my life also have been important mentors and partners in my success.

Many colleagues have given me important direction and guidance over the years. In 1987, for example, I was invited by one of the top financial advisors in our firm, George McLeod, to join him as a junior partner. For five years we worked together every day, and throughout that time our business did very well and I learned a great deal that would later contribute to my professional success. I learned what a person in the top 3 percent of his industry dresses like, how he thinks about investing, his strategies for investing with high-net-worth clients, and his feelings about his own success. I unknowingly gained exposure to a culture of success, simply through my daily contact and experience with George.

At work, partnerships help sustain momentum by enabling each individual to exercise his or her own strongest skill set, while ensuring that *all* essential aspects of the business are running smoothly. In 2001, I made a decision that I needed a business partner, and I eventually hired Susan Naylor—who turned out to be just the right person for my business. Susan and I, while alike in some ways, are completely different in our skill sets. I am a dreamer and a visionary, a salesperson, and a number cruncher. My job is to stay in touch with our clients, to meet face-to-face with them, and to ensure that our investment strategies are on track to meet their investment goals. I easily become distracted or bored with repetitive projects, and I can lose my focus. Susan's job is to make sure our business is running efficiently. Susan, is task oriented, detail driven. She loves to start and finish a project without taking a breath. She has a high attention span and an incredible memory for the minutest detail. She is the queen of customer service. If she says it is going to be done, then it is going to be done. I encourage you to find quality partners who complement your weaknesses.

I encourage you to find good partners and to take every opportunity to benefit from their support and advice in all aspects of your life. If you feel that you can use even more targeted advice and guidance, it is a great idea to hire an executive coach. Typically, an executive coach helps you clarify your own goals, and then offers systematic activities each week to help encourage you to reach those goals. Would it be a good investment to hire someone that could exponentially launch your career forward? What if you are making $30,000 a year and you want to make $50,000? What if you are making $50,000 and you want to make $100,000, or you want to boost your salary from $100,000 to $250,000? An executive coach can help make that change happen much more quickly, so your investment in this service might repay itself many times over.

Investing Time and Thought in Long-Term Planning

Momentum can change direction, and it can do so relatively quickly. This means that your long-term goals must guide every task, every action, of every day. Growth is only positive when it is taking you in your chosen direction. Momentum can take you toward your long-term goals, but you have to keep your eye on those goals every day, and adjust the course of your journey whenever necessary.

In my company, we are all committed to growing our knowledge and skills, and to using our understanding of our business to remain on course. Our long-term planning includes monthly networking events and teaching seminars. Everyone in our team takes an active role in community events. We do not just attend community events, either; many of us have taken time to become leaders in community organizations, and all of us regularly volunteer our time and skills to their programs. Our active involvement with our community is essential in guiding our continued growth and success. It helps us remember our starting point, it reinforces our strategy and story, it feeds our growth as an organization, and it helps keep our organization moving in the direction of our long-term goals. Every volunteer action you make counts. Every kindness you show to someone else, every service that you deliver, every part of your life that you give to others, pushes your flywheel and takes you to a higher level of personal and professional achievement.

Micro-Action: Consider the Direction of Your Own Momentum

Which way is momentum carrying you in your life? Anyone can temporarily wander off course or enter a periodic downward spiral, but we do not have to submit to being dragged further and further from our goals. We have to look for specific things we can do to change direction and get back on track. This chapter helps you understand where you are today and where you want to be in the future; I shared with you my personal experiences in managing change, along with some concrete micro-actions designed to help you hit your own goals. As the final micro-action in this chapter, take a moment to consider where you are in your life, where you want to go, and what positive actions you are taking to make sure that you continue heading in that direction.

Micro-Action

. . . .

Take five minutes now, to explore the answers to these questions:

- Does your business strategy create a strong and memorable identity?

- Does it tell a story that differentiates you from your competitors?

- Have you put into place processes and systems that can keep building the momentum of your change?

- Have you strengthened your ability to continue to grow through drawing upon the knowledge of mentors and forming useful and sustaining partnerships?

Remember the decision to change happens in an instant, but putting the wheels of that change into motion takes persistent effort. Yes, you can decide today that you will be physically fit or make the decision to stop smoking, but then, you have to begin moving down the path of daily—and lifelong—

change. Each of us must continue changing, day after day, to become a different person and to use the momentum of each day's successes to power us on through a lifetime of growth and development.

6

. . . .

Pushing Past the One-Yard Line and Breaking through to Peak Performance

I am a sports fan, and one of the sports I love the most is football. What could be more exciting than watching a team catch the ball at one end of the field and, through a series of well-planned plays and incredible bursts of effort, move the ball down the field, past their opponents, and into the end zone? After many years of watching the game, however, I have begun to think that when a team lands on their opponent's one-yard line—99 yards down the field and just 36 inches from scoring a touchdown—something mysterious happens. The defense gets stronger, and the offense seems to grow more nervous. Maybe that last yard feels more like 100 yards to the offensive team. I have no statistical data to back me up in this observation, but I have seen it time and time again; if the offense makes a first down on the one-yard line with three plays left, they sometimes have incredible difficulty moving the ball into the end zone. Imagine the disappointment these players must feel, realizing they have to settle for less, simply because they could not push past the one-yard line and on to success.

This phenomenon is not limited to football, either. Common wisdom in the business community says that although many executives can move a project to 98 percent of completion, only a few actually finish the last 2 percent successfully. I see this "2 Percent Rule" at work all the time; people achieve true success and growth in their business or personal life, only to stop short of fully accomplishing their goals. They do well, but they never quite live up to their full potential; they just cannot seem to push past the "one-yard line" that separates them from peak performance.

We all struggle from time to time with the one-yard line or the 2 Percent Rule. We have a report due and we are "almost" finished except for that one remaining piece of research. A week later, the report remains "almost" finished. At home, we diligently work on an outdoor cleanup project for weeks and finish everything but replacing that one broken light fixture; one year later, the broken light fixture is still in place.

In life, as in football, winning matters. No matter how much energy, effort, and attention we devote to getting "almost" there, if we fall short of achieving our goals we never enjoy the satisfaction and fulfillment that comes with true success. Even though we ran 99 yards, if we cannot move past the one-yard line toward our own peak performance, we have to settle for less. In these situations, strong-armed opponents rarely hold us back. Instead, through lack of confidence, commitment, strategy, and action, we create our own one-yard-line barriers that prevent us from fully realizing the promise of our potential.

You do not have to settle for less than full success. Throughout this book, you have learned a number of important ideas and actions for building toward personal and professional success. This chapter offers you a set of ideas and tools to help boost your performance to higher levels that have proven to be successful for those who attend my workshops and seminars. The 7 Minute Ideas and micro-actions you will learn in this chapter help you destroy the self-defeating barriers of inaction, indecision, insecurity, and unpreparedness that can prevent you from reaching your own end zone of success. The tools and techniques in this chapter will help you with these important tasks:

- Refocusing on your purpose and vision

- Assessing your room for growth

- Living your mission

- Setting aggressive one-yard-line goals, such as re-emphasizing essentials, improving systems, gaining competence, and tracking daily progress

- Building and using one-yard-line resources

- Embracing the power of perseverance

In every organization, only a portion of the people achieve real success. Those people who make it to the top are those who have torn down the artificial barriers of procrastination and in-decision to push through the one-yard line and into the end zone. You can be one of those people, too.

Realigning Your Purpose, Vision, and Mission

In chapter 1, we talked about the purpose of discovering—and being guided by—your purpose in life. As I said, your pur-pose defines what you want to accomplish with your life and how, in the process of accomplishing it, you serve others. With-out purpose, we are lost, floating through life without direction, and with little hope of arriving at any given destination. Our purpose fuels our dreams, guides our actions, and defines our vision and mission in life. Remember the 7 Minute Idea I offered to you earlier:

· · · · ·

By aligning your choices, priorities, and dreams, you direct your actions toward achieving your goals and fulfilling your purpose.

· · · · ·

One thing that causes many people to find themselves stuck on the one-yard line of success is an abandonment of purpose. If you find yourself at a standstill in your personal or professional journey toward excellence, you should stop and ask yourself if you have remained true to your life's purpose:

- Are you putting your purpose as a leader, teacher, mentor, caregiver, listener, healer, organizer, or supporter to work?

- Do your goals, beliefs, and actions align with your purpose?

- Does your vision accurately reflect your purpose or do you need to expand your vision to encompass a bigger and bolder mission in life?

· · · · ·

What we do for others is often what brings us the greatest joy and fulfillment in life.

· · · · ·

This is an important 7 Minute Idea. If your purpose truly guides your work, you will remain driven to achieve success. You will feel compelled to keep moving toward the achievement of your mission, but not by guilt, greed, or ego. The sheer joy of fulfilling your purpose will propel you toward success.

Assessing Your Room for Growth

Do you remember the story I told you earlier about the farmer who placed a jar over a pumpkin blossom? The pumpkin grew to fill the walls of the jar then stopped. It could have become much larger and more beautiful, but the limitations imposed by that thin glass barrier confined its growth. Your vision can limit you in the same way. If you find that you are falling short of achieving your full potential, you might need to expand your vision to encompass a bigger mission and more far-reaching goals.

Micro-Action: Assess Your Skill Sets

Early in this book, you set goals for improving your knowledge base, creating and following a written action plan, improving your organizational skills, and other important tasks involved in pursuing your purpose. This next micro-action can help you assess how much progress you have made toward achieving those goals, and how much room for growth remains:

Micro-Action

· ·

Take ten minutes to complete the following self-assessment of your current skill sets.

Based on the scores you assign to your performance in each area, determine the five areas in which you need to make the most improvement. Next to each listing, record one action you will take to improve in that area.

TABLE 6.1

	NEEDS IMPROVEMENT			EXCELLENT SKILLS	
	1	**2**	**3**	**4**	**5**
Understanding Your Purpose					
Goal Setting					
Belief in Your Ability					
Organizational Skills					
Technology Skills					
Communication Skills					
Marketing Skills					
Creativity					
Public Speaking					
Networking					
Finding New Prospects					
Differentiation from Competition					
General Knowledge					
Product Knowledge					
Historical Market Knowledge					

The Five Areas That Need the Most Improvement:	Action:
1. _____	_____
2. _____	_____
3. _____	_____
4. _____	_____
5. _____	_____

If you find that you are not interested in improving in the areas listed above, then you need to determine how critical those areas are to your purpose, vision, and mission. If you find that you have no interest in improving in an area that is critical to the fulfillment of your purpose in life, then you need to re-evaluate your commitment to that purpose. Otherwise, begin tackling the improvements you listed. Do not make this process overwhelming and difficult; choose actions that can make an immediate improvement in your skill sets and self-image.

Living Your Mission

Back in the 1990s, I attended numerous conferences and seminars in which I was asked to write my "mission statement." I always did just that, drafting several enthusiastic paragraphs that I felt accurately and completely described my mission in life. Then, I read *The Path,* by Laurie Beth Jones. In that book, Jones said we should be able to recite our mission statement at gunpoint and have a fifth grade student understand it. As I read on, I realized that a mission statement is not some complex, binding document you should frame and hang on your wall. A *real* mission statement is etched in your heart—a simple statement of your life's purpose.

Here is mine: *My mission is to educate, motivate, and encourage.* I know that in order to fulfill my purpose I have to live my mission. What about you, are you living your mission? If you reach a point where you cannot seem to progress any further down your current path, you might want to stop and look around to see how your journey might have strayed from your original mission.

Micro-Action: Discover Your Mission

As with your purpose, your mission is already etched in your heart. To discover your mission fully, however, you need to articulate that "inner knowledge" as a complete and understandable statement. In discovering your mission, you need to ask yourself a series of questions: What hopes, dreams, activities make your heart pound and your palms sweat? What do you love most? What drives you? What makes you willing to push through the tough times? The answers to these questions help you articulate your mission.

You may find it helpful to write down a series of individual words that embody your passion. A micro-action that can help with that process:

Micro-Action

. . . .

Take five minutes to read through the words in the following list and identify those that are connected to your mission in life. Then, on the lines in the next page, create your own list of terms that you might use to describe your mission.

educate	peace	vision
motivate	patience	clarify
encourage	kindness	strategic
love	teach	prioritize
hope	play	organize
joy	serve	simplify
work	feed	team
passion	lead	follow
creativity	advocate	flexible
faith	health	write

Drawing upon the terms in the previous lists, and other words that are important to you, take a moment now to write your mission statement here:

_____

_____

_____

_____

_____

_____

As you review your choices in the above mission statement, what can you discover about yourself? Are you including activities that support these actions in your daily life? If not, you may not be working to fulfill your purpose. Find your purpose, understand it, and live guided by it. Your mission should become the measure of your life. With a stronger understanding of your mission, you can maintain simplicity and balance in your life, and begin to *live it*.

Setting One-Yard-Line Goals

If you find yourself butting your head against one-yard-line barriers to success, you might need to set some more aggressive goals in order to push through and destroy those barriers. As the years pass by in our jobs, it is easy to lose sight of some of the most important daily activities that contribute to our personal and professional growth. The "daily-ness" of our lives distracts us and we focus on the easier, less-risky tasks ahead, rather than tackling new challenges. Sometimes our satisfaction with past successes can make us complacent—or just plain lazy. When that happens, we stop growing and moving toward the fulfillment of our larger dreams and ultimate purpose. If you are stuck at the one-yard line, now is the time to commit to setting bigger, more challenging, and more aggressive goals for pushing through to true success. I call these one-yard-line goals.

As a financial advisor, for example, I have made a one-yard-line goal to attempt to contact 25 people per day. If, at the end of the day, I only made 24 calls, I am still stuck on the one-yard line. There is no touchdown for me, unless I complete that one final call to hit my one-yard-line goal. Trust me, there are days that I do not want to make 25 telephone calls. There are days that I just want to read e-mail and sit around and chat with my friends or maybe call one or two clients. If I want to truly push myself to move closer to my larger dreams and purpose, though, I have to pick up the phone and call 25 people every day. I can tell you the "every day" part of that commitment is the most difficult to fulfill.

Another of my one-yard-line goals is to host at least five face-to-face client appointments every week. That means that I need to meet with one client every day to review their personal holdings. I established this goal because our clients let us know that they want to see us; they want to be in personal contact with the people who manage their money. (For clients who live out of town, we often host these meetings via a telephone conference.) That is just one more way I push myself to new levels of success. If I host four appointments a week, I remain on the one-yard line; if I host five appointments, I land in the end zone—touchdown!

Another one-yard-line goal is that I attempt to read one book a week—and not just fluff books, either. This week, I finished *Benjamin Franklin: An American Life,* by Walter Isaacson. This book was not easy for me to get through, but I learned a great deal in the process. I learned about Franklin's virtues and his inventions, his successes, and his failures. I recognized in him some behaviors that I would like to emulate, and I learned he had some beliefs I do not agree with at all. It was fascinating to step back in history into Franklin's world and walk those paths with him. Every book, every week, improves my understanding of my job, my life, and the world around me; in other words, it pushes me closer to success.

What are your one-yard-line goals going to be? What one-yard goals would make a difference in your life? Consider these ideas:

- Could you accomplish 5 percent more by increasing your activity level at work every day?

- Could you handwrite two, three, four, or maybe even five thank-you notes a day to your best customers telling them how important they are to you?

- Could you create forms and procedures for frequent tasks within your business, both to make your life easier and to free up more of your time at work for activities related to growth rather than maintenance?

- Are you willing to take 15 minutes at the end of every day to create a written plan of action for the next day?

- Can you push yourself to make sure that your business strategies are truly creating the story and image that you want to project?

If you are ready to be different tomorrow than you are today, you need to determine what your "nonnegotiable" daily business activities are and then set them as your personal one-yard-line goals.

Micro-Action: Set Your Goals

This next micro-action will help you in the task of determining and setting your goals:

Micro-Action

. . . .

Take ten minutes right now to set some one-yard-line goals. Then, every day, check the list to determine whether you have made it to the end zone.

TABLE 6.2

ONE-YARD-LINE GOALS	YES	NO
1.		
2.		
3.		
4.		
5.		
6.		
7.		

Successes do not just evolve; they are created. You have an incredible opportunity to identify and move beyond the artificial barriers that stand between you and peak performance. By setting and pursuing aggressive one-yard-line goals, you can achieve success and change the path of your destiny. Working with one-yard-line goals means your success becomes a simple choice and every day you decide if you win or lose. Choose your "nonnegotiables" and then act on them every day.

Improving Your Competence

One of the first techniques you can use to push past the one-yard line is to become more competent. Competence can make all of the difference in your world. As you read earlier, I raised the bar on my own life over the past four years by attempting to read or listen to one book every week. Reading is an important method for gaining competence in *any* industry, but it is rarely the only one. What goals would help you become more competent in your industry? Perhaps you can commit to increasing the number of training seminars you attend each year, or to attaining new certifications in one or more areas of your business. Maybe the first commitment you can make is to limit the amount of television you watch and give yourself time to learn more about the work you do and the customers you serve.

Do not forget the importance of using mentors to improve your competence. Anyone who has skills and experience that you do not have can serve as your mentor. Your mentor might be a manager who is one level above you. If you are a middle manager in a corporation, you could find successful mentors among the other middle managers of different areas of your corporation. You might even find a mentor in another field entirely who has successfully managed issues or technologies that could improve your competence in your own business.

I routinely seek out people who are more successful than I am and ask them to share their approach to business with me. Sometimes I schedule phone conferences with these mentors. Other times, I travel alone or with my team members to spend time at the mentor's office viewing firsthand how the office is set up, how they run their business, and the marketing tools they use. If I am attending an industry conference, I always try to find out ahead of time what top performers in my industry will be attending. Then, I e-mail these people in the weeks before the conference to ask if I can schedule a breakfast or lunch meeting with them. During those meetings, I ask them specific questions about how they achieved their success. I ask them about how they schedule their day, how their offices are staffed, how they conduct their training and on-going education, what specific technologies they use, what systems they have in place, even what ideas or actions they've tried that haven't worked. It is amazing what you can learn during lunch with a superstar in your own industry. These conferences give me an ideal time to learn from and begin to emulate those people who have already pushed past the one-yard line.

Successfully using a mentor requires only that you find out what others do well, and then apply that knowledge and those techniques in your area. Committing to a specific reading goal only requires that you get a library card and take the time to begin using it. If you find yourself stuck and unable to cross the line to true success, your first plan of attack should be to improve your competence.

Improving Your Processes and Systems

Remember that creating and using good working systems enables you to invest more time and attention in *growth* rather than *maintenance*. Nevertheless, even the best systems need periodic review and updating. If you find that you are stuck in your personal or professional growth, you might have outgrown the systems that once worked well for you. When we devote time to developing working systems, it is easy to fall into the habit of using them without evaluating their ongoing effectiveness as our business grows and changes. When our systems become inadequate, we once again spend too much time reinventing basic processes each time we perform certain tasks. As a result, we have less time to devote to growing in our skills, knowledge, and pursuit of service. Remember this 7 Minute Idea:

· · · · ·

Your processes and systems drive the basic functions of your business; if your systems are out of date, your business cannot reach peak performance.

· · · · ·

Here are some important processes and systems you might currently be using in your own business:

- *Employee training.* One of the best investments for any business with multiple employees is to create written training guidelines and policies for all of your employees. Your best advertising is an employee who is friendly, helpful, and confident in selling your products or services. Training is a repeatable process that makes you different from everyone else. After you develop an employee-training process, you must remember to revisit it regularly to be sure it remains up-to-date and effective.

- *Contact management software.* As you learned in Chapter 5, my team fully implemented a contact and customer management program called ACT! to help us manage our daily client contacts and keep track of our ongoing customer commitments. Contact management software offers you endless opportunities for systematizing the processes in your business; from printing out daily schedules, to providing new-account processes and on-going contact reminders. The requirements for these processes can change over time and software updates continually offer new opportunities for improving contact management processes. Be sure your contact management software is up-to-date and providing the types of processes and forms you need *now.*

- *New client orientation processes and materials.* New clients benefit from a quick orientation of your business and its services. Your business might provide this information through a New Client Orientation booklet, which highlights what your customers should expect to receive from doing business with you. Your booklet might cover information such as directions to your office and parking availability, explanations of how often you will be in contact with your clients, listings of the types of services you provide, and an outline of what customers should expect when doing business with you. Your business specifics and client needs change over time, so review and update these materials and processes regularly.

Micro-Action: Review Your Existing Systems

Even if you think your systems are in top shape, I encourage you to complete this next micro-action:

Micro-Action

. . . .

Take five minutes right now to answer these questions:

- Are all of your basic processes—order fulfillment, client contacts, reports, scheduling—systematized?

- Are you up-to-date on the latest technologies for customer care and service processes?

- Have you developed any new systems within the past year? Two years?

- Do you have any nonsystemized processes within your organization? Could they be systemized?

No matter how successful you are in systematizing your processes, you should never consider that you have taken your systems as far as they can go. Customer needs change, business practices change, new competition arises, and technologies advance. By remaining on top of changes in those areas, you'll be better able to keep your systems up-to-date. As a result, your business can continue to grow, rather than allow time-consuming, outdated processes to hold it back. Consistently ask yourself, "Where will our business need to be in five years?" Some of the one-yard-line goals that can help you make sure your systems are evolving and your business can continue developing are as follows:

- Subscribe to journals, reports, and white papers carrying industry updates

- Network to stay abreast of system developments in other businesses

- Participate in at least two conferences/seminars each year devoted to exploring ways to improve processes and systems in your field

Tracking Your Progress

In an earlier chapter, I shared with you my ideas about the importance of setting daily goals. I also told you that I make it a practice to take about ten minutes at the end of each workday to list my top priorities for the next day. Now, I want to urge you to recommit to adopting this practice, every day. Many times, as we begin to achieve success in our business, we neglect some of the important habits and processes that served as our first stepping-stones to success. If your professional growth has slowed down, if you find that you are simply unable to break through to achieve your vision and fulfill your purpose, you can overcome this obstacle by paying closer attention to your daily goals and progress.

Constructing a daily action plan helps to reaffirm your commitment to fulfilling your purpose. Reading that list each morning provides structure for the day ahead, and sets up real, attainable milestones. If you achieve nothing else but the items recorded on your list, you can leave work knowing that you accomplished the top priorities you had set for yourself that day. I believe that following a daily action plan is one of your strongest tools for pushing through to peak performance.

Micro-Action: Keep a Written Daily Progress Report

If you have had trouble committing to writing and following a daily action plan, you might want to consider this micro-action:

Micro-Action

. . . .

Create and use a written daily progress report.

To make this process as simple as possible, I encourage you to use a form like the one I included in Figure 6.1 (this form can also be found in the Appendix and a full size version can be downloaded from our Web site, http://www.TheSevenMinute Difference.com). This is a two-sided sheet that allows you to do several things on one piece of paper. You can

- list six or seven top priorities for the next day;

- record what times you arrive at and leave work;

FIGURE 6.1

Daily Progress Report

Date
M T W T F
Arrived
Left

My Purpose

Top Three Personal Goals
1.
2.
3.

Tasks
1.
2.
3.
4.
5.
6.
7.
9.
10.
11.
12.
13.
14.
15.

Top Priorities
1.
2.
3.
4.
5.
6.
7.

Thank You Notes Written
1.
2.
3.
4.
5.

Notes

© Seven Minutes, Inc. 2006

FIGURE 6.1 (continued)

Voice Mail

name	number	call time
		message

name	number	call time
		message

name	number	call time
		message

name	number	call time
		message

name	number	call time
		message

name	number	call time
		message

name	number	call time
		message

name	number	call time
		message

name	number	call time
		message

name	number	call time
		message

© Seven Minutes, Inc. 2006

- write down your purpose (mission statement) every day as a reminder

- record your top three personal goals;

- track how many thank-you notes you write every day;

- keep a short "To Do" list and a record of daily notes and accomplishments; and

- use the back of the report to record all of your daily incoming voice mail messages and mark them off as you return them.

Keep all of your daily progress reports in a three-ring binder for future reference. Keeping this type of daily progress helps systematize the way you do business. Maintaining a written daily progress report keeps you more organized and on top of the daily activities that are vital to pushing through to peak performance.

Giving Yourself Permission to Succeed

Often, in business, I see people that I know could be successful, but who almost seem to have a fear of success. They are afraid to go past the tipping point of some success to *true* success. Sometimes these people have suffered some sort of disappointment in life or experienced circumstances that hold them back. Those stumbling blocks are inevitable in any life, but at some point, we have to wake up and realize that we all face disappointment every day. We cannot use setbacks as an excuse to stop trying to move forward and we cannot define ourselves by our disappointments or use our fear of success to limit our growth. We must push through disappointment and overcome our circumstances to achieve our ultimate goals. We must give ourselves permission to succeed.

The one-yard line of "almost successful" is not a fun place to be. You know that you are close to making it, close to pushing past the point where life could become more interesting. Yet, you sit there watching life pass you by, day by day. There it goes, another day. Until one day, you wake up and you say, "You know what? I deserve more than this." Something happens in your heart and your life begins to change. You begin to undertake every day with pleasure and anticipation, and you willingly channel your time and energy into the things that matter most to you. Whether you realize it or not, you have given yourself permission to succeed. Then, one day you look around and realize that you are there—you are in the end zone, operating at peak performance, and enjoying the life you always envisioned. When I experienced this day in my life, I immediately understood the dance football players perform when they score a touchdown. It is not cockiness—it is absolute exultation.

Let me be clear, landing in the end zone and finding fulfillment has nothing to do with how much money you make or how impressive your new title sounds. *Landing in the end zone occurs the moment you discover that your purpose and your life's activities match up.* When the heartbeat of what drives you is in rhythm with your daily life, you have reached your own personal end zone. If you feel that life is never quite enough, like a child with her nose pressed on the toy store window, looking in but never entering, ask yourself this question: What is holding you back? Could it be your nonproductive work habits, your negative illusions, your reluctance to strive for something that you are not certain you can achieve? If so, only *you* can tear down those artificial one-yard-line barriers and give yourself permission to cross over into the end zone of success.

Micro-Action: Discover Whether You Invest Your Time in Success

How do you spend the hours of your day? Are you working toward crossing the one-yard line or are you simply repeating the same mistakes that have you stalled just short of that goal? Try this micro-action to help you give yourself permission to break stagnant, nonproductive routines and use your time to actively move toward your goal:

Micro-Action
. . . .
Take ten minutes to record the major activities of your typical work week on the form on the next page, indicating how you spend blocks of time each day.

FIGURE 6.2

TIME	MON	TUE	WED	THU	FRI	SAT	SUN
6:00 AM							
6:30 AM							
7:00 AM							
7:30 AM							
8:00 AM							
8:30 AM							
9:00 AM							
9:30 AM							
10:00 AM							
10:30 AM							
11:00 AM							
11:30 AM							
12:00 PM							
12:30 PM							
1:00 PM							
1:30 PM							
2:00 PM							
2:30 PM							
3:00 PM							
3:30 PM							
4:00 PM							
4:30 PM							
5:00 PM							
6:00 PM							
7:00 PM							
8:00 PM							
9:00 PM							
10:00 PM							
11:00 PM							
12:00 PM							

If you have weekly meetings, block them out; if you spend the first hour of every morning checking your e-mail, mark that time out on the schedule. Try to create a complete picture of your typical workweek.

Now, take a hard look at how you invest your time. Are the events or activities that occupy significant blocks of your time giving you a meaningful return? If not, now is the time to give yourself permission to drop those activities from your life and move on to new and better ones. Even if your schedule was especially productive six months or one year ago, it might not have kept pace with the changing reality of your personal or professional life. Remember, you cannot change your life by repeating the same mistakes day after day.

When you find yourself stuck in your growth, I encourage you to use the ideas discussed here to set aggressive goals and exploit all available resources to push through to success. Give yourself permission to succeed, and then commit gladly to the tasks that will take you there. Do not be confined by fear, hesitation, or doubt; break through those artificial barriers to grow fully into your destiny.

Remembering That Everything Matters

"Everything matters." That is the motto of Keith Kessinger, coach of the Arkansas State University baseball team. His father, Don Kessinger, was the famous Chicago Cub, St. Louis Cardinal, and Chicago White Sox player, who played in the major leagues for 15 years. Before joining ASU, Kessinger played in the minor league for seven years and briefly in the major league. At every practice, Kessinger expects the best. He expects every ounce of effort, and he demands that his team members focus on every detail. These men are competitors; Kessinger's primary responsibility, as their coach, is to make them *winners.* They must believe that they are winners, they must play like winners, and they must act like winners at all times. To help them reach that goal, he frequently offers them his strongest words of encouragement: "Everything matters." Every action of every member of the team contributes to the team's identity and image. Every at bat, every pitch, every defensive moment—everything matters. When Kessinger's players know that *everything* they do affects their ability to succeed, they focus on excellence in every action.

In business today, it can often be said, "Nothing matters." We show up late for work. Many times, even when we are at the office physically, our minds wander continually to other places and interests. We are tired, overwhelmed, with no agenda and no reason to work. Our dreams have died and we do not care. Many of us hover listlessly on the one-yard line in this state, just within reach of our success.

If you are not using every resource available to you to reach your ultimate success, then nothing that you do—no matter how difficult, expensive, or brilliant it may be—will help you break through that one-yard line. This is an important 7 Minute Idea:

. . . . .

In striving to reach excellence, either everything matters or nothing matters.

. . . . .

Embracing the Power of Perseverance

There is one final 7 Minute Idea I would like for you to remember:

. . . . .

If you want to be different tomorrow than you are today, persevere.

. . . . .

Too many people grow complacent just before they reach the end zone; they quit striving just before they hit their goals. Do not stop short of your success—persevere.

You might be closer to achieving your goals and living your dreams than you realize. If you have been stuck on the one-yard line, now is the time to look deep inside your actions, motivations, and ideas, and make the effort to begin moving forward again. The ideas in this chapter—and in this book—do not rely on massive investments or instant makeovers in your lifestyle.

They simply require you to choose to make small incremental changes in your daily work habits.

These ideas can help you hone your business strategy, story, systems, and processes. Use them as a springboard to exploring the resources unique to your own industry and situation—the "seeds of change" that can take you toward the fulfillment of your personal and professional destinies.

7

Life-Changing Decisions, Life-Changing Actions

This book has been an exploration of the process of change. I want you to pay special attention to that word—"process." Although the decision to change itself represents the first step on a journey of transformation, the process of change unfolds over time. In fact, we can only reach our finest goals, realize our biggest dreams, and fulfill our true purpose by embracing change as a constant condition of our lives.

. . . . .

In other words, change happens in an instant,
and takes a lifetime.

. . . . .

This is good news for anyone who has grown discouraged by the slow progress of past attempts to make some fundamental change. Change is not a finite event. It is not something you should be able to complete on a timetable. Real change reveals its benefits slowly. People rarely go from poor to rich in a period of 6 weeks, or from having a horrible job to a stellar career in 2 months, or from being overweight and out of shape to being perfectly fit within 90 days. More importantly, on the extremely rare occasions when people *do* experience radical changes quickly—they win the lottery, are discovered by a talent scout, or lose weight rapidly through dramatic diets, pills, or procedures—they can rarely sustain and build upon the benefits resulting from that change. They blow the money, their career fizzles out, or they lapse into old habits and the weight comes back. Lasting change is a lifelong process of *growing*. When you grow, you are doing more than just changing behaviors—you are nurturing stronger beliefs, different attitudes, richer desires, and deeper convictions.

There comes a point where we realize that we want more—that we want to become different, become more tomorrow than we are today. The trigger for your decision to change may be your relationship with your spouse, your spiritual life, your weight or health, or your job or current level of competency. When some aspect of your life is out of step with your goals, dreams, and purpose, you *can* make the decision today to change. That is the moment when your change begins. You might not feel or see the change—it does not necessarily signal its arrival with some great epiphany, but you have set the wheels of change in motion and, like our comparison to the flywheel, they will start to gain momentum.

The decision to change gives you permission to dream, to imagine, and to believe you can be different. Imagine yourself in the future. Then, imagine utilizing your energy to become that person, to lead a better, richer, and much more enjoyable life. What a glorious reality. For change to follow, however, your decision must grow from deep within your soul and carry your convictions with it. Life-changing decisions require life-changing actions.

If the decision to change launches you on your path to life-long development, the following forces will propel you along that path and toward the fulfillment of your purpose:

- Appreciation for things that matter

- Acceptance of the power of your mind

- Investment in your passion

- Replenishment of your energy

- Belief in hopes and dreams

- Celebration of victories

- Commitment to continual growth

Unlocking the power of these tools can propel you to initiate change in your life, and to walk down the path of that change with conviction and commitment. I hope these ideas will help you shift your focus from past false starts at meaningful change to stepping out confidently on your own personal journey of growth and development. You might be just heartbeats away from achieving more, becoming more, and enjoying more. Take the time to think deeply about each of these tools. They represent the life-changing actions that can carry you on to your destiny.

Pursuing the Things That Matter

Make the decision to change and you change. Isn't that great news? How many of us have been stuck in situations we disliked? How many times have you wanted to be different, but you felt trapped by your circumstances? Now is a wonderful time to decide what you want out of life and then to begin changing your actions to achieve that goal.

As I wrote this book, I came to some surprising decisions about my own goals. I first conceived of this book as a "business book"; I began writing strictly with the goal of motivating you to do better in your business. I included plenty of concrete ideas and action steps to help you improve your personal productivity, grow your career, and even make an impact on your entire company. In writing the first chapter of the book, however, I quickly typed up a list of my own goals to participate in a micro-action I was describing. I regularly list my goals and I find that they change and develop over time. As I glanced at this list, something interesting struck me: only two of the seven goals I listed involved increasing my wealth or improving my position at work. Then, I went on to draft quickly a new priorities list, as well. Wow! On an eight-item list, only my hobbies rank as a lower priority than my job and my finances. Therefore, I decided that I *would* write this book to encourage and inspire you, but not necessarily for you to become rich or gain a big promotion. The most important thing I hope I have inspired you to do in this book is to *recognize and pursue the things that matter most to you in your life.* I believe that when you pursue goals related to your personal success, you typically advance closer to achieving your professional goals, as well.

Isn't it interesting that we spend the first part of our lives chasing a dream built primarily on the concept of accumulating money? We invest a lot of time and energy stressing over our annual salary, our network, our title, our power, our status. None of those things are totally inconsequential and there is nothing wrong with striving for success. As I age, however, I am discovering that my most important decisions have never revolved around how successful I am in my career or how much money I make. Certainly, my most recent life-changing decisions have nothing to do with propelling me to the next rung on the ladder of success. My decisions are growing out of what is most important to me: my spiritual development, my family and friends, my health, and then—coming in last place—my business. My desire to succeed in my vocation still drives me; my work is incredibly important to me. I just know that I cannot invest the majority of my time, energy, and effort in the pursuit of professional success. My spiritual growth, family, friends, and health matter much more to me and will *always* receive the majority of my focus and effort. Interestingly enough, as I have focused more of my attention on my personal purposes and priorities, my business has become even more successful.

Go back and review the goals and priorities you listed in chapter 1, and remember to redraft your goals list regularly. As you practice this daily reminder, ask yourself whether you are investing the majority of your life—your hopes, your efforts, your energy—in the things that matter most to you. To achieve meaningful growth, you need to align your energies with your priorities. If you spend your life chasing hollow trophies, in the end you will discover that they lead you to one deadend after another. Let the things that *really* matter to you be the guideposts through your ongoing journey of development.

Unleashing the Power of Your Mind

Your mind holds all of the power necessary to propel you toward your goals. You may have heard the expression "If you can believe it, you can achieve it." I know that statement is true. Nothing can take you farther or make more of a difference in your life than the incredible power of your own mind.

Let me show you what I mean. Take a brief glance at the picture of lemons below.

Now, stare at this picture for a moment. As you do, imagine holding one of the lemons in your left hand. Feel the texture of the skin, feel the weight of the fruit in your palm. Now imagine cutting into the lemon and slicing it into perfect wedges. Next, imagine picking up one of the lemon wedges and holding it close to your nose. Smell the lemon deeply. Finally, imagine biting into the lemon wedge.

FIGURE 7.1

What happened to your mouth when you thought about biting into the lemon? If you are like me, you received a big burst of saliva through your mouth as though you had just experienced a tart, sour taste. Your body responded with a physical reaction to a purely mental cue; your mind said, "you taste something sour—salivate!" and your body obeyed.

Of course, in reality, you cannot feel, touch, or taste those lemons—they are only images on a page. All of those sensations, along with sight and hearing, registered in your brain, though. Therefore, your body reacts to the world based on the directions your brain gives it. Everything you feed your brain influences your actions, ideas, and your state of being. Realizing that, we should be alarmed at the results of studies that show the average American household watches five to eight hours of television per day! Think about what our brains absorb during those hours: tabloid news, violent television shows, mind-numbing sitcoms, celebrity gossip, and endless, repetitive advertisements. If we feed our brain violence, pettiness, hopelessness, and consumerism, can you imagine how our bodies respond? Do we want to condition our minds to believe they exist in a world of negativity, greed, and despair? Our beliefs become our reality, and our lives unfold accordingly.

Of course, many of the negative things reflected on television and in the weekly tabloids really do exist. I do not accept, however, that they define the world we live in. Our world is so much bigger, and better, and more complex than the two-dimensional reflection of a television screen. I choose to feed my brain a more balanced diet. 15 minutes of news in the morning, 15 minutes at night, and many hours spent talking with my family, reading good books, traveling, visiting with my friends, living through my faith, and enjoying my hobbies. For every nasty, frightening, negative reality in this world, there are a hundred bright, shining, positive treasures that are equally real and infinitely more nourishing— both intellectually and spiritually.

Our brains are more powerful than any of us truly knows. I believe saying positive statements aloud, visualizing the outcome with your eyes, and embedding future expectations in your conscious and subconscious mind will put the wheels of change in motion and make those expectations a reality. According to John Maxwell's audio series, titled *How to Make Personal Changes*, there are six steps that we go through in the process of changing thought into reality:

1. *Thought.* As I noted earlier, if you think it, you can live it. We have to think about whom we want to become, what path is most likely to take us there, and what we might have to sacrifice along the way.

2. *Belief.* If we want to be different tomorrow than we are today, we must believe we can become different. We also must believe in the direction we have chosen for our life, and our ability to make the journey.

3. *Expectation.* Expectation causes our energy level to rise and releases adrenaline into our system. Although it begins as a purely mental phenomenon, expectation triggers a physical reaction. Expect the best, and harness the power of your expectations.

4. *Attitude.* Having a positive attitude means facing every circumstance head on and pushing through with character, dignity, and integrity. I believe the old saying that successful people are willing to do what unsuccessful people are *not.* Your attitude is a mighty tool for dealing with challenges and making the most of opportunities.

5. *Behavior.* Your behavior is an outward reflection of your inward thoughts, beliefs, expectations, and attitudes. Therefore, as you become more positive and proactive in each of those areas, your behavior will improve accordingly.

6. *Performance.* Your performance provides a daily measuring stick of your personal growth and development. I am happy to say, your performance is one of the easiest things to improve. If you were inconsiderate yesterday, you can become kinder and more thoughtful today. If you overslept today, you can get up on time tomorrow.

Micro-Action: Feeding Your Mind with Positive Images

What kinds of images, thoughts, and ideas are you feeding *your* brain? Because, believe me, they reflect in everything you do; the way you look, your attitudes, your beliefs, your accomplishments. Your mind is busy creating your reality, so what kinds of tools and building materials are you supplying it?

If we wake up every morning saying, "I can be more today than I was yesterday," paying attention to the good things in our lives, and expecting that today is going to be better than yesterday, then we have set the stage for that expectation to come true.

Here are some things to tell yourself every day. Try this micro-action:

Micro-Action

· ·

When you wake up in the morning, read the following statement out loud:

"My purpose in life is to serve others and make their lives better. I have been given wonderful gifts and talents and I have the courage today to 'paint the canvas' of my life. I am blessed beyond measure and today I will be grateful and enjoy my life."

As you read the statement, visualize each of the positive things you mention. See yourself taking action, walking into your office happy and energized, enjoying a healthy lunch, accomplishing the day's goals, and returning home with joy to spend the evening laughing with your family or friends, reading a good book, working in your garden, playing the piano, refinishing furniture, or doing anything that contributes to making your world a better, more pleasant place to be. Try to vividly imagine these positive events unfolding as you read the statement, and hold them in your mind for a few minutes after you finish reading.

I challenge you to try this micro-action every morning for two weeks. If you develop a different positive statement with which you would like to greet the morning, by all means, use it! The important thing is to experience the power of beginning every day with optimism and a positive plan.

You cannot predict or control the future, but you have great power to influence your own journey through life. I encourage you to nourish your mind and actively envision the positive and productive life you want to live. Your mind is the most powerful part of your body, so care for it well—make good use of it!

Remaining True to Your Passion

Throughout this book, I have emphasized the importance of following your passion. It does not matter what business you are in or how you spend your day—whether you are a corporate CEO, a financial advisor, a stay-at-home parent, a full-time volunteer, a minister, a doctor, or a retiree—you will not find true happiness and success in your daily life if you are not driven and guided by your passion. So often, the people who attend my workshops tell me that they have great difficulty finding passion in their working lives. How can you be passionate about a cubicle, a computer, and lunch at your desk? Well, I can tell you that the first step in that process is to take some time to recognize the passion that you actually feel about anything. When you recognize and acknowledge your passions, you can find amazing ways in your life to embrace them. Let me give you an example.

I am very passionate about spending holidays with my family. I love my family very much, and I love going home to my extended family at Christmastime. My husband and I get up early, wake the children, then pack up the car and make the three-hour drive to my hometown. Even as I turn on to the street of my childhood home, I begin to feel the excitement. I am still blocks away, but when I see my parents' house my heart rate quickens. I walk up to the door and I can already smell Christmas dinner cooking. Just the aroma of that roasting turkey makes my heart beat even faster. Then, the door swings open, my mom and dad greet me with smiles and shouts of pleasure and hugs, and as I hold them in my arms, my pleasure deepens. We spend the day chattering, reminiscing, listening to the children laugh, and sharing my mother's lovingly prepared dinner, and I remember all the reasons that I love this experience so passionately.

I want to feel as passionate about what I do in my daily life as I feel about those holiday dinners in my parents' home. When we share food, and memories, and laughter with those around us, all of our senses engage, and the pleasures we experience can link directly to our deepest passions.

One of the ways that we can experience those pleasures more deeply in our daily work lives is to involve as many of our senses throughout the day as possible. Life is too short to work eight, nine, ten hours a day simply putting in time at a job. Every hour of your day is an hour of your life—you cannot afford to leave your passions at home when you head for work each morning! Of course, if we discover that we have lost all passion for our work, then we might need to pursue a different path entirely. However, often we can find many opportunities to acknowledge and rekindle our passions within the job we have right now.

If you are a leader in your business, you are in a prime position to put passion back into your workplace. Enliven your employees by engaging their senses. Be willing to order lunch or share a potluck meal with your co-workers. Pat them on the back and tell them they are doing a great job. Pop some popcorn and let the smell fill your office and then personally deliver bags to your employees. Bring a CD player to your next staff meeting and have some of your employees' favorite music blaring as they walk in to the meeting. Even if you are not the one in charge, you can certainly leave a note of encouragement at a co-worker's desk for a job well done, you can bring a Crock-Pot of chili to share, or you can be the one to instigate a community activity.

As you bring pleasure to others, you may rediscover your passion for the work you do.

We are all passionate about something in life, whether that passion revolves around family, art, music, sports, reading, traveling, or any other source of pleasure. Your passion might involve standing in freezing water up to your waist with a fly rod in your hands, donating your time and energy to working with the homeless and hungry in your community, or an unlimited number of other possibilities. There is something in your life that gives you a feeling nothing else can deliver. Think deeply about what stirs your heart and soul, what it is about the things you enjoy most that kindles your passion. Then, begin working to acknowledge opportunities for those passions throughout your day. Discover your passions and then give them the time they deserve. Remain true to your passions and your life will grow richer every day.

Allowing "Air" Into Your Life

I believe that we all need "air" in our life. Everyone knows what air is—an essential element, oxygen, life itself—but I am using the term here in a special sense.

I have made it a personal goal to try to drink at least 60 ounces of water each day. Regardless of where you find me—the car, my desk, my home—I usually have a bottle of water nearby. I was sitting at a stoplight recently and picked up my ever-handy bottle of water, unscrewed the top, and took a drink. Then, just for fun, I pushed the rim of the bottle tightly against my lips and tried to continue drinking. With no space for air to enter the bottle's opening, I could not draw much water into my mouth. Instead, I only succeeded in creating a vacuum that held the water away from me and was even a little bit uncomfortable for my lips.

At that moment, a flash of inspiration hit me. Just as I needed that tiny gap between my upper lip and the bottle opening to allow air into the bottle so the water could flow into my mouth, I needed gaps in my work life to allow "air" into my life so I could be more productive. When we cut all of our free time—time spent with our families, friends, and hobbies—our work takes on the same pressure we experience when we try to suck water out of a sealed bottle. The laws of physics dictate that air must enter the bottle to replace the space the water occupied; otherwise, we create a vacuum. In the same way, without the opportunities to replace the energy we expend on our jobs—without allowing "air" into our lives—our productivity comes to a standstill.

"Air" is something that replenishes your energy, and in that regard, it can vary for each person. Some things are essential for us all; we replenish ourselves by getting enough rest, eating healthy food, and exercising, but those are just the baseline ingredients. I experience "air" in my life when I watch my daughter swing from the limb of a magnolia tree in our backyard or when I sit in a lawn chair surrounded by friends at my son's baseball game. I replenish myself with "air" as I hold my husband in my arms and tell him I love him, and when I call my mother and father to just talk. I bring "air" into my life when I climb in bed with a good book.

"Air" is not a luxury reserved for your personal life, either. While going from one meeting to the next may be necessary, if you truly want to be different tomorrow than you are today, you need to build time for renewal and replenishment into your daily work schedule. For some readers, you may want to schedule an hour a day to read, write, or reflect. For others, you may want to schedule an entire day away from the office once a month. The important 7 Minute Idea you need to remember here is this:

· · · · ·

If you do not replenish your energies, you will soon run out.

· · · · ·

While only you know what brings "air" into your life, I can assure you that you need it. Replenishing your life is not an optional activity; you must do it in order to revive your spirit, heal life's bruises, and feed your optimism. All too often, we squeeze breathing room out of our life and then wonder why we feel dead. Bring back the "air" in your life.

New Leaves

My purpose in life revolves around the concept of "growing." I want to grow personally and I want to encourage others to grow. In nature, growth is a cycle. Consider the vast oak tree; each spring, it bursts forth in a full bloom of new, tender, green leaves. Throughout the summer, the leaves gather sunlight and process it into vital nutrients that help the tree grow taller, stouter, and healthier. As autumn arrives, the leaves slowly fade in a brilliant display of color, changing from green to orange, then fall from the tree. The mighty oak's branches remain bare until the following spring, when the cycle begins again. Without the loss of old growth, no new growth would be possible.

The same kind of renewal is necessary for personal ongoing cycles of growth and development. I have come to realize that I cannot do everything in life. Some of the things that once were critically important to my personal or professional growth need to fall away, so I can encounter new challenges, develop new ideas, and experience new things. Occasionally, I need to shake the tree and allow some of the "old leaves" to fall off and make room for new growth. We all need to be willing to occasionally shed old practices and make way for new growth in our lives.

So many people's lives are full of "dead leaves." They cling to old ideas, hurts, bitterness, anger, tension, and stress out of sheer habit, even though those familiar feelings hold them back in their ability to grow and be happy and fulfilled. Other habits can be even harder to break—continuing to perform old routines that are no longer productive, failing to delegate work that no longer needs personal participation, clinging to practices that have ceased to produce the benefits they once offered. Even when we sense that long-held feelings, habits, and activities are actually holding us back rather than feeding our growth, we hang on to them as precious treasures, refusing to simply let go. It is easy to litter our lives with these "dead leaves"; but once identified, we can give ourselves permission to let them fall from the tree.

Like some of the other ideas in this book, getting rid of "dead leaves" is a simple decision of will. To achieve new growth and make true advances toward our purpose, we need to be willing to shed our old leaves and remain bare for a while, as our new growth blossoms forth. Once freed of counterproductive habits, outdated ideas, and negative feelings, we create room in our lives for new ideas to form, new habits to grow, and new depths of joy, kindness, forgiveness, love, and peace to develop.

Periodically, think about your need for new growth, and determine which of your old practices or beliefs might be preventing you from achieving it. Then, make the decision to drop those obstacles from your life, and give yourself some time to discover what new aspects of your life will grow to replace them.

Feeding Your Hopes and Dreams

To be different tomorrow you must reignite your hopes and dreams. Children are the best dreamers. I look my children in the eye and ask, "What would you like to be?" My nine-year-old daughter quickly replies, "I want to be an artist, a fashion designer, and a stay-at-home mom." My eight-year-old son looks puzzled for a moment and then says, "I don't know, Mom . . . I guess I want to be either a drummer or a basketball player." The great thing about children's dreams is that they are usually in perfect alignment with their current gifts and skills. My daughter is already a talented artist and she loves children. She will be a fabulous artist, fashion designer, and mom. My son probably does not know or care how good he is in math yet, but he knows he loves music of all kinds and he would rather be playing basketball than almost anything else in life.

As parents, we work hard to encourage our children to follow their dreams. We take them to special lessons and classes and offer them every opportunity for growth that we can manage. Yet, all of us have faced some disappointing moment in life in which we drifted away from our dreams. Reality sets in, and we recognize that we may not be able to pay the bills as an artist or as a drummer, or we grow tired of trying. We may find we simply cannot stare down our fear of failure, so we allow our dreams to die.

You need to reawaken the artist, the drummer, the explorer, or the writer who lived inside you when your dreams were young. It is not too late! Bring your old drum set down from the attic and start practicing again. Sit down in front of the computer and begin writing the next great American novel. Take that art class at the community college. One of my clients took a month away from her family to travel to Italy to study art—she was 75 when she took up painting! Nothing brings us more pleasure than reviving and respecting our hopes and dreams.

Dreams are like magnets, they draw us closer to what once seemed impossible. Dreams can only happen, though, when we give ourselves time to develop them and the freedom to believe in them. What secret dreams lie hidden in your heart? Do you want to be a poet, a singer, or an artist? Do you have the idea for an invention? Have you been harboring the outline of the next bestselling book? What tiny thoughts keep creeping back into your mind when you least expect them? Now is the time to stop suffocating your dreams. Live a little more, step outside the boundaries you have drawn around your life. Dreams may exist first in your mind, but they do not need to stay trapped there. Bring them into the light and enjoy their pleasures.

Creating Olympic Moments in Your Life

I love watching the summer Olympics. I appreciate watching athletes who have trained for years—maybe all of their lives—for one moment in time. These people have discovered their strengths and they have focused their entire lives around the pursuit of that single goal. They have one strategy, one niche, one event, and they have come to this one moment in time to pursue their dreams.

The 10,000 meter race is my favorite event to watch. Men and women from all over the world compete. If they make it to the finals, they have proven their ability, and now are poised to run the most important race of their life. These eight men or eight women get down in the blocks and the whole world goes silent. The gun goes off, and all eight contenders begin to run full blast, 10,000 meters, 6.2 miles.

I cannot imagine what it must feel like to run like that in front of millions of viewers, knowing this is what you have trained your whole life for, and that your lifetime of effort is now on the line and unfolding before the world. Round and round they go, sweat pouring, muscles pulling, every ounce of their body hurting. Yet I do not believe they feel that pain. While athletes are "in the zone," I do not think they experience anything except complete and total abandon and joy. They are doing what they were called to do. They are investing everything in their dream and living totally in the moment.

They are not worrying about yesterday's practice, paying the electric bill, or spending their first big endorsement if they win the race. They are totally focused on running as fast and as well as they can at that very moment.

This kind of joy is not available only to Olympic athletes. By doing the best that we can do and investing ourselves fully in the job before us, we all can experience life's "Olympic moments." I savor the Olympic moments of my life, moments where I experienced complete abandon, where my joy was so intense I could literally feel it sweeping over me. I can recall three such moments from my past: The first of these is the moment I walked down the aisle, grabbed my husband's hand, looked into his eyes, and said "I do." Another occurred about three years later, when my daughter was born and I held her in my arms for the very first time. The third followed about a year and a half after that, when my son was born. He was so tiny—five pounds six ounces—and when I felt his breath against my cheek, I knew that we had both shared the victory of that powerful Olympic moment.

After I came to understand my purpose in life and began pursuing it with all of the passion, energy, and strength I could muster, I realized that living life to the fullest is about having Olympic moments every day. Feeling pride in finishing a difficult project, finding a way to give your family an unexpected pleasure, ticking off the last item from your daily goals list—when our days are fueled by our passions, we live each of them "in the moment."

Most of us occasionally endure some form of pain in our daily work life. Dealing with co-workers, hitting budgets, meeting projections, making tough decisions on hiring and firing— any of these common events in a typical workday can be unpleasant and difficult. Yet I still urge you to run with abandon. Give yourself fully to the task at hand. Put your training, energy, and strengths on the line, and do your job with everything you have to give at that moment. When you fully invest yourself in whatever task you undertake, you experience more joy, you win more victories, and you suffer less pain.

When the 10,000 meter race is over, three people win medals, but every one of those people that ran the race achieved their dreams. We do not always have to come out on top to live life to the fullest; but we do have to run the race. We have to run with joy, passion, and hope if we want to experience life's Olympic moments.

Do not only seek out Olympic moments in your own life; actively work to help those around you experience more Olympic moments in their own lives. Make a special call to your children, write a love note to your spouse, surprise your parents with a visit, or plan a dream vacation. Life is short; look for every opportunity to experience it richly.

Extending Your Reach

Stretching your body is a great way to refresh tired muscles, pull your joints back into proper alignment, improve your breathing and heart rate, and boost your circulation. Stretching, in fact, improves our overall sense of well-being, and helps prepare our muscles for strenuous work. When we stretch both before and after hard work or exercise, our muscles work better and suffer less damage. Most of us already know the therapeutic value of stretching, but I am emphasizing it here because I want you to consider the equally important benefits of stretching our capabilities by reaching for higher goals.

To illustrate the uses of this final developmental tool, I would like you to take both of your arms and stretch them high above your head. Seriously, put the book in your lap and stretch your arms as high as you can above your head. Doesn't that feel great? Now, try to extend your reach by stretching your arms just a little higher; dig deep for even half an inch more. When we think we have stretched to our limit, most of us can extend a tiny bit more. Alright, put your arms down, and take a few minutes to think about how you have just proved to yourself that you can extend your reach; you can always grow just a little bit more.

This is the final developmental tool: a willingness to dig deeper and extend your reach. Most of us believe that we live our lives to the best of our ability; we are the best son, daughter, wife, husband, friend, business partner, co-worker, employee, and/or boss we can be. We do what is asked of us and we enjoy moments of happiness and pleasure, but, often, we know something is lacking. We want MORE—more out of our marriage, or friendships, or jobs, or life in general. Well, you can *have more* out of any or all of those things, simply by being willing to stretch, to extend your reach and continue growing.

To help you get more out of your life, I am going to place the responsibility for doing so right back on your shoulders. If you want to be different tomorrow than you are today, choose to be different, then begin tackling the small changes that will *make* you different. If you want more out of your marriage, grab your spouse today and tell them, "I loved you when I married you, and I love you now. I want more out of our relationship and I am willing to do whatever it takes to bring back the joy and the love we once shared." If you want more out of your job, sit down and spend some time truly discovering where you are, how you got here, where you want to go, and the best path for undertaking that journey. Whatever it is that you want, just reach for it.

When I asked you to stretch as far as you could, you did. When I asked you to stretch just a tiny bit more, you did that, too. That small extra distance in your reach is the essence of this 7 Minute Idea:

· · · · ·

Dig deeper, try harder, and be willing to believe in your ability to do more, and you will do more.

· · · · ·

The true sweetness of life lies just beyond the ordinary effort. The difference between a life of mere existence and a life of passion and joy is just a tiny stretch away. I am not asking you to put down this book and then make a huge change in your life. I am asking you to be slightly different tomorrow than you are today. Then, to be slightly different the next day and slightly different the next—until you become who you were created to become.

When you wake up and realize you can live a purpose-filled life, full of knowledge and passion, then you will experience incredible joy and want nothing more than to share that joy with others. You will find your purpose and begin to live it, and you will have made the most important difference possible in your life.

In or Out?

Change really does happen in an instant. It happens the moment you decide to change. Now that decision is yours to make—either you are *In* or you are *Out*. It is that simple. The earth does not have to shake nor does lightning have to flash across the sky. You simply draw a line in the sand and you say,

"Today, I choose to be different." You can decide right now to begin the wonderful process of growing into your true self.

Decide to be *In*. Once you make that decision from your heart, your life will never be the same. Change happens in an instant, it happens the moment you decide to change.

As the author of *The 7 Minute Difference*, I can tell you with confidence, "I'M IN!" My hope is your life will be filled with much joy, hope, and love as you continue to discover how the smallest decisions can have a huge impact on your life—seven minutes at a time.

Appendix

· ·

Resources and Recommended Reading

Guide to 7 Minute Ideas
and Micro-Actions

Guide to Recommended Reading

The following reading list includes some of my favorite books, organized by category. These books have helped me grow toward my own personal and professional fulfillment, and I hope they help you in the same way.

Business Concepts

Good to Great: Why Some Companies Make the Leap and Others Don't
HarperBusiness, 2001
James C. Collins

The E-Myth Revisited: Why Most Small Businesses Don't Work and What to Do About It
Collins, 2001
Michael E. Gerber

Think and Grow Rich
Aventine Press, 2004
Napoleon Hill

Marketing

Selling the Invisible: A Field Guide to Modern Marketing
Warner Books, 1997
Harry Beckwith

The Invisible Touch: The Four Keys to Modern Marketing
Warner Books, 2000
Harry Beckwith

What Clients Love: A Field Guide to Growing Your Business
Warner Books, 2003
Harry Beckwith

The Tipping Point: How Little Things Can Make a Big Difference
Little Brown, 2000
Malcolm Gladwell

Blink: The Power of Thinking without Thinking
Little Brown, 2005
Malcolm Gladwell

Positioning: The Battle for Your Mind
McGraw-Hill, 2000
Al Ries, Jack Trout

Fish: A Remarkable Way to Boost Morale and Improve Results
Hyperion, 2000
Stephen C. Lundin, et al

The New Positioning: The Latest on the World's #1 Business Strategy
McGraw-Hill, 1996
Jack Trout with Steve Rivkin

Networking

Marketing to the Affluent
McGraw-Hill, 1997
Thomas J. Stanley

The Millionaire Next Door
Simon & Schuster, 2000
Thomas J. Stanley

The Millionaire Mind
Andrews McMeel Publishing, 2001
Thomas J. Stanley

Motivational

*Be Quick, but Don't Hurry!: Finding Success in the
Teachings of a Lifetime*
Simon & Schuster, 2001
Andrew Hill, John Wooden

*The Path: Creating Your Mission Statement
for Work and for Life*
Hyperion, 1996
Laurie Beth Jones

The Greatest Salesman in the World
Bantam Books, 1983
Og Mandino

*Earl Nightingale's Greatest Discovery: Six Words That Changed the
Author's Life Can Ensure Success to Anyone Who Uses Them*
Dodd, Mead, 1987
Earl Nightingale

The Strangest Secret
Keys Company, 1999
Earl Nightingale

PowerTalk!: The Six Master Steps to Change
Audio Renaissance, 1994
Anthony Robbins

The Art of Exceptional Living
Nightingale-Conant, 2003
Jim Rohn

Goals! How to Get Everything You Want—Faster Than You Every Thought Possible
Berrett-Koehler, 2003
Brian Tracy

TurboCoach: A Powerful System for Achieving Breakthrough Career Success
Amacon, 2005
Brian Tracy with Campbell Fraser

The Prayer of Jabez: Breaking Through to the Blessed Life
Thorndike Press, 2004
Bruce Wilkinson

Allegories

The Wealthy Barber: Everyone's Commonsense Guide to Becoming Financially Independent
Random House, 1998
David Chilton

The Richest Man in Babylon
Signet, 1988
George S. Clason

Who Moved My Cheese: An Amazing Way to Deal with Change in Your Work and in Your Life
G.P. Putnam's Sons, 1998
Spencer Johnson, Kenneth H. Blanchard

Customer Service

Raving Fans: A Revolutionary Approach to Customer Service
William Morrow, 1993
Ken Blanchard, Sheldon Bowles

Gung Ho! Turn On the People in Any Organization
William Morrow, 1998
Ken Blanchard, Sheldon Bowles

Becoming a Category of One: How Extraordinary Companies Transcend Commodity and Defy Comparison
John Wiley and Sons, 2003
Joe Calloway

Body Language

How to Say It at Work: Putting Yourself Across with Power Words, Phrases, Body Language, and Communication Secrets
Prentice Hall, 1998
Jack Griffin

Signals: How to Use Body Language for Power, Success, and Love
Bantam Books, reissue edition, 1984
Allan Pease

Personal Development

How to Win Friends & Influence People (rev.)
Galahad Books, 1998
Dale Carnegie

The Five Love Languages: How to Express Heartfelt Commitment to Your Mate
Northfield Publishers, 1995
Gary Chapman

Time Management

Getting Things Done: The Art of Stress-Free Productivity
Penguin Books, 2003
David Allen

Simplify Your Work Life: Ways to Change the Way You Work So You Have More Time to Live
Hyperion, 2001
Elaine St. James

Investing

Smart Couples Finish Rich: 9 Steps to Creating a Rich Future for You and Your Partner
Broadway Books, 2001
David Bach

Smart Women Finish Rich: 9 Steps to Achieving Financial Security and Funding Your Dreams
Broadway Books, 2002
David Bach

Start Late Finish Rich: A No-Fail Plan for Achieving Financial Freedom at Any Age
Broadway Books, 2005
David Bach

The Art of Asset Allocation: Asset Allocation Priniciples and Investment Strategies for Any Market
McGraw-Hill, 2003
David M. Darst

Rich Dad, Poor Dad: What the Rich Teach Their Kids about Money—That the Poor and Middle Class Do Not
Warner Business Books, 2000
Robert T. Kiyosaki, Sharon L. Lechter

The Million Dollar Car and $250,000 Pizza
Dearborn Trade, 2000
Allyson Lewis

A Random Walk Down Wall Street (Eighth Edition)
W. W. Norton and Company, 2003
Burton G. Malkiel

Stocks for the Long Run: The Definitive Guide to Financial Market Returns and Long-Term Investment Strategies (3rd Edition)
McGraw-Hill, 2002
Jeremy J. Siegel

The Future for Investors: Why the Tried and the True Triumph Over the Bold and the New
Crown Business, 2005
Jeremy J. Siegel

History/Biography

D-Day: June 6, 1944: The Climactic Battle of World War II
Simon & Schuster, 1994
Stephen E. Ambrose

Undaunted Courage: Meriwether Lewis, Thomas Jefferson, and the Opening of the American West
Simon & Schuster, 1996
Stephen E. Ambrose

Lincoln, the Unknown
World's Work Ltd., 1947
Dale Carnegie

Benjamin Franklin: An American Life
Simon & Schuster, 2003
Walter Issacson

Endurance: Shackleton's Incredible Voyage
Carroll and Graf, 1999
Alfred Lansing

John Adams
Simon and Schuster, 2001
David McCullough

Shackleton's Way: Leadership Lessons from the Great Antarctic Explorer
Penguin Books 2002
Margot Morrell, Stephanie Capparell

Additional Resources

Remember, you alone have control of your time. You owe it to yourself to identify and use any timesaving technology or resource that fits your working needs and style. Whether you use standardized forms, the latest MP3 player and audio books, or a simple kitchen timer, every second you save helps you move closer to crossing the one-yard line into your ultimate success.

Forms for Correspondence

Whenever possible, try to stay away from form letters. Use these examples for your handwritten thank-you notes and correspondence. Make sure you hand address the envelope and, whenever possible, use nonstandard size notecards and postage stamps.

- Periodically, I send out a thank-you note to existing clients, just to remind them that I appreciate their business:

> Dear _____:
>
> There is absolutely no reason for writing this letter other than to say **thank you**. Thank you for your business and the confidence you have placed in us. It is a pleasure doing business with you and I consider you one of my valued clients.
>
> If you have any questions, please let me know. I am here to be of service to you. Thanks again for the opportunity to earn your trust and confidence.
>
> With Warmest Regards,
>
> *Allyson Lewis*

- I also have a shorter thank-you note that I use for the same purpose:

> Dear _____:
>
> I just wanted to write you a quick thank-you note for your time today. We appreciate your confidence, your friendship, and your business. Please let us know whenever we can be of service to you.
>
> Thanks again.
>
> Sincerely,
>
> *Allyson Lewis*

- After my first meeting with a potential client, I send this note:

> Dear _____ :
>
> It was a pleasure meeting with you today. I sincerely appreciate the opportunity you have given me and someday soon, we hope to be able to call you a client.
>
> Thank you for your consideration and I look forward to talking with you soon. In the meantime, please do not hesitate to call should you have any additional questions.
>
> Sincerely,
>
> *Allyson Lewis*

- When someone refers a new client to my business, I send the referrer this thank-you note:

> Dear _____ :
>
> I wanted to take this opportunity to personally thank you for referring _____ to us. I feel honored that you are comfortable enough with the level of service we provide and with me to recommend us to others. There is no better feeling than the one that comes from having a satisfied client who refers us to their friends.
>
> We appreciate your confidence, your friendship, and your business. Please let me know if we can ever be of service to you. Thank you again.
>
> Sincerely,
>
> *Allyson Lewis*

A Library Card

Go to your public library and acquire a library card. A library card is a free resource that can save you a great deal of time and money in pursuing an active plan of reading. Instead of having to shop for and store 52 books every year, I can use my library card to maintain my reading goal of one book per week. I can locate books immediately; if the library does not have a book I need, they can order it and notify me when it has arrived. Because I can only keep the books for a limited amount of time, the library also helps me maintain a schedule for my reading and for starting and finishing books quickly.

A library card also gives you access to another important time-saving tool—audio books. The public library acquires or uses inter-library loan to provide almost any audio series that you ask for. Then, you can listen to these books in your car, or while doing housework, or while exercising.

An MP3 Player and Audio-Book Source

You might remember that in a previous chapter I spoke to you about using an MP3 player to listen to audio books downloaded from the Internet. Consider acquiring some kind of technology for listening to audio books. I have personally invested in an Apple iPod, but there are less expensive MP3 players that work as well for downloading and listening to books on tape. You can download these with a subscription to

a service such as http://www.audible.com. This service is another important time-saving technology that has helped me
advance my competence. For a small monthly charge, I can
download two books every month. Again, this schedule helps
to keep me on track with my reading goals. Regardless of
which type of technology you prefer, I have found that listening to audio books on tape is a wonderfully easy way to
save time while pursuing an active reading plan for improving
my competence.

A Notebook

I am a huge user of technology, but sometimes nothing is
better than a tiny, black leather notebook. A notebook offers a
simple, fast, and portable way to record important ideas and
thoughts. It is a growth-enhancing tool, as well as a time-saving
technique. You can use any kind of notebook that works best
for you; to record my ideas and important thoughts, I use a
Moleskine notebook. It has a sturdy leather cover and is small
enough to carry with me wherever I go (you can learn more
about Moleskine at http://www.moleskine.co.uk).

Ideas are gifts and our memories can barely hold a conscious thought for more than seven minutes. When an idea hits
you, you want to have something nearby to write it down in. I
use my notebook almost every day. When a thought hits me, I
write it in my Moleskine notebook. When I remember an
"open loop" that needs to be closed, I write it in my Moleskine
notebook. If you carry a notebook with you, you never need to

worry about losing a valuable thought or idea—no matter how quickly your mind might wander away from it.

A Kitchen Timer

Another important time-saving resource that I use is a simple kitchen timer like the one shown below. Although it may seem like a low-tech approach to time management, I have found that this timer is one of the most effective tools I have for using my time wisely.

I originally purchased the timer because I absolutely refuse to be late for appointments and other deadlines, and I wanted a physical reminder to help me stay on time. When I need to

FIGURE A.1

leave the office in an hour, for example, I set the clock for about 45 minutes (this type of timer counts backwards) and then I work with my head down straight through until the timer goes off. I do not have to check my watch every five minutes to be sure I am not running late. I can remain focused on the task at hand and depend on my handy timer to let me know when it is time to leave.

I have found other great uses for this tool, as well. If I am working on a big project, and I think it is going to take two or three hours, then I bring my kitchen timer into play. Working straight through on a single project for two hours can become mind numbing, so I set my timer for an hour. Then, I turn off my phone, turn off my e-mail, put my head down, and work until the timer goes off. I do not allow anything to break my concentration until then. When the timer beeps, I stand up, stretch, get a drink of water, check e-mail and voice-mail messages, or attend to any other pressing business. Then, I set the timer for another hour and go back to work. In addition to helping me lose myself in my work, while remaining fresh and productive, I often find that I am able to accomplish much more in each hour that I work. Often, I can complete a job that I estimated as a two-hour project in a single hour, simply because I have concentrated fully on the project during that time.

Grocery List

You have already seen the Daily Progress Report, the Goals List, and the Weekly Time Planner. Now, here is another of my favorite time-saving lists—the Grocery Store List. At my home, a copy of this list resides on the kitchen counter; when someone realizes that we need to restock our pantry with an item, he or she simply circles it on the list. This list organizes items as the grocery aisles typically group them, so you can save yourself the aggravation of walking back and forth throughout the store. For proper credit, my good friend Tenny Brown shared the grocery store list concept with me. This, and all of our other forms, is available for downloading and editing from our Web site at http://www.TheSevenMinuteDifference.com.

BATHROOM
Alcohol
Peroxide
Antibiotic cream
Band-Aids*
Deodorant
Shampoo
Conditioner
Soap
Lotion
Eye drops
Hair gel
Bath soap
Multivitamin
Hairspray
Q-tips*
Razors
Shaving cream
Toothbrush
Toothpaste
Mouth rinse
Tylenol*
Ibuprofen
Aspirin
Cold medicine
Antibacterial handsoap
Wet Ones*

CHILD DEPT.
Baby bath
Baby lotion
Baby powder
Diapers
Formula
Wipes
Baby food
Cereal
Baby
shampoo/conditioner
Small/big pony tail
holders
Socks

CLEANING
Detergent
Stain remover
Dishwashing liquid
Tilex*
Brillo* Pads
Sponges
Dryer sheets
Formula 409*
Clean up spray
Clean up wipes
Lysol*
Lysol* kitchen
Toilet bowl cleaner
Rags
Gloves
Mop
Windex*
Buckets
Furniture polish
Kitchen cleaner

CAN FRUIT
Peaches
Pineapples
Applesauce
Fruit cocktail

DAIRY
American cheese/slices
Biscuits
Crescent rolls
Cinnamon rolls
Margarine tub
Margarine stick
Butter stick
Cheddar cheese block
Cheddar cheese shredded
Cream cheese
Eggs
Whole milk gallon
Skim milk ½ gallon
Mozzarella cheese
Sour cream
Whipped cream
Dips
Choc. Chip Cookie Dough

SOFT DRINKS
12-pack coke/pepsi
12-pack diet coke
12-pack root beer
2-liter
Cola
Diet cola
Dr. Pepper*
Sprite*
Bottled water big/little
Sparkling water

SNACK FOODS
Oreos*
Choc. Chip cookies
Pringles*
Fritos* big/ little
Cheetos* big/little
Goldfish* crackers
Graham crackers
Pretzels
Popcorn
  Butter
  Natural
Potato chips
Ruffles*
Ritz* crackers
Saltine crackers
Snack mix
Tortilla chips
Salsa

CEREAL
Apple Jacks*
Total*
Raisin Bran*
Smart Start*
Cheerios*
Syrup
Pop-tarts*
Fruit Loops*
Cereal bars
Frosted Flakes*
Granola bars
Oatmeal
Fruit Snacks

BAKING GOODS
Flour
Baking powder
Baking soda
Brown sugar
Chocolate chips
Corn starch
Nuts
Oil
Pepper
Powdered sugar
Salt
Shortening
Spices
Jell-O*
Pudding
Sugar
Vanilla
Pam* spray
Sprinkles
Food coloring
Brownie mix
Cake mix/ frosting

JUICE
Gatorade* red/green
Kool-Aid*
Cranberry
Grape
Apple
Juice boxes

RICE AND PASTA
Bouillon
  Beef
  Chicken
Cooking wine
Spaghetti sauce
Gravy mixes
  Brown
  White
Macaroni & Cheese
Shells & Cheese
Other pasta
Elbow noodles
Spaghetti
White rice
Minute Rice*

CAN VEGETABLES
Creamed corn
Green beans
Mushrooms
Spinach
Beets
Parmesan cheese
Peas
Corn
Tomatoes 28/14.5
Jalapeños
Tomato sauce
Whole new potatoes
Sliced new potatoes
French fried onions
Whole kernel corn
Baby green beans
Baby corn
Lima beans
Kidney beans

CONDIMENTS
Caesar dressing
Croutons
Vinegar
Italian dressing
Mayonnaise
Mustard
Catsup
Ranch dressing
French-Italian-Thousand
Relish
Salsa
Pickles whole/baby/ chips
Olives

BREAD
Grape jelly
Honey
Hotdog buns
Jam
Peanut butter
Wheat/white bread
Dinner rolls
French bread
Garlic bread

SOUP
Chili w/beans
Chili no beans
Vegetable
Chicken noodle
Beef broth
Chicken broth
French onion soup
Mushroom soup
Cream of chicken

FROZEN FOODS
Ice cream sandwiches
Juice bars
Frozen pizza
Ice cream
Orange juice/ lemon juice
Popsicles
Whipped cream
Frozen corn
Chicken nuggets
Frozen lasagna
Hash browns
Broccoli spears
Chicken pot pie
Fish sticks
Waffles

FRUITS
Apples
Bag apples
Bananas
Cantaloupe
Grapes
Lemons
Oranges
Peaches
Strawberries
Watermelon

CANDY
Chocolates
Licorice
Gum/mints
Hard candy

VEGETABLES
Baby carrots
Bag lettuce
Cilantro
Celery
Broccoli
Carrots
Corn
Lettuce
Mushrooms
Onions
Potatoes
Tomatoes

MEAT
Chicken breasts
Fully cooked chicken
breasts
Chicken legs
Chicken nuggets
Hot dogs
Ground beef
Steak-rib-eye/filet/t-bone/
Sirloin/pot roast
Pork chops
Bacon
Spiral cut ham
Frozen hamburgers
Fajita meat
  Chicken
  Beef
Deli
  Turkey/ ham/
  American white
Lunchables*

TRASH BAGS
13 gallon
30 gallon
compactor bags

STORAGE
Foil
Plastic cups
Saran* wrap
Ziploc*
  Gallon/freezer
  Gallon/storage
  Quart/ freezer
  Quart/ storage
Snack
Coat hangers

PAPER PRODUCTS
Kleenex*
Paper towels
Toilet paper
Travel Kleenex*
Paper plates
Paper napkins
Paper cups

MISCELLANEOUS
Pictures/ film
Greeting card
Tape
Dog food/cat food
Light bulbs 40-75-100
Girl b-day present
Boy b-day present

Daily Progress Report

Date

M T W T F

My Purpose

Arrived

Left

Top Three Personal Goals
1.
2.
3.

Tasks
1.
2.
3.
4.
5.
6.
7.
9.
10.
11.
12.
13.
14.
15.

Top Priorities
1.
2.
3.
4.
5.
6.
7.

Thank You Notes Written
1.
2.
3.
4.
5.

Notes

© Seven Minutes, Inc. 2006

Voice Mail

☑

name	number	call time
		message

name	number	call time
		message

name	number	call time
		message

name	number	call time
		message

name	number	call time
		message

name	number	call time
		message

name	number	call time
		message

name	number	call time
		message

name	number	call time
		message

name	number	call time
		message

Index